STUDYING FILMS

ALSO AVAILABLE IN THIS SERIES

STUDYING THE BOURNE ULTIMATUM

Neil Archer

Dedication

For my Dad, who recommended this film; Giulia, who watched it with me; Noa, who might watch it one day.

First published in 2012 by
Auteur, 24 Hartwell Crescent, Leighton Buzzard LU7 1NP
www.auteur.co.uk

Copyright © Auteur Publishing 2012

Designed and set by Nikki Hamlett at Cassels Design www.casselsdesign.co.uk

Printed and bound by Short Run Press Ltd, Exeter, UK

British Library Cataloguing-in-Publication Data
A catalogue record for this book is available from the British Library

ISBN: 978-1-906733-59-9

Contents

Chapter One: A Serious Blockbuster?

It draws many of its themes and images directly from the headlines and from our paranoid zeitgeist, including waterboarding ... black ops, rogue intelligence outfits with sinister agendas, CIA snatch-squads operating on foreign soil, extraordinary renditions and state-sanctioned murder.[1]

The best blockbuster of the summer... and the standard to which future blockbusters should be held.[2]

Fig 1: "This Summer, Bourne Comes Home": poster image for The Bourne Ultimatum

The above quotations both refer to the same film: *The Bourne Ultimatum* (2007) (Fig 1); the third in the series of action thrillers that began in 2002 with *The Bourne Identity*, and continued with 2004's *The Bourne Supremacy*. At first glance, this might seem surprising. The idea of the traditional summer blockbuster that we have come to know, and maybe love, does not usually conjure up the kind of images suggested above: torture, regime change, covert espionage and political assassination. These ideas and images seem removed from the comic-book thrills and alternate universes of today's popular movies. While we might expect to hear about them on the evening news, they are hardly what most of us choose to see on a Friday night. Yet *Empire*, the UK's biggest-selling movie magazine, begs to differ. *The Bourne Ultimatum*, it suggests, is not just a blockbuster; it is a *serious* blockbuster.

How we define 'blockbuster' itself is not exactly straightforward, but common opinion suggests that it is a film that makes a lot of money. Yet these days, with film websites and news media promoting studio trailers months before a film comes out, we have got used to hearing about blockbusters *in advance*. This is in fact not a new phenomenon: Hollywood studios have been concentrating their resources on specific, pre-planned blockbuster or 'event' movies since the 1960s, banking on these particular big-budget films – known in the business as 'tentpole' films – to prop up the rest of the studio's less bankable output.[3]

The Bourne Ultimatum appears to fit the bill on both fronts. It cost Universal Pictures, one of Hollywood's oldest studios, over $100 million to produce. Released in August, traditionally one of the highest-grossing times for movies, it was Universal's stand-alone hit of the summer, figuring in the end of year US box-office top ten at number seven, and making over $400 million in worldwide receipts.

Quite what we might understand by a 'serious blockbuster' will be the subject of this first chapter; how we relate it to *The Bourne Ultimatum*, meanwhile, will be one of the main considerations of this book. In thinking about a 'serious blockbuster', it's worth pointing out from the start that I'm making use of a double meaning. One definition of serious, according to the Oxford English Dictionary, gives us 'important, deserving consideration'. We can apply this definition, then, to things that make a significant impression: so significant that we have no choice but to take them seriously. As an example, let's take two of director Steven Spielberg's hugely successful 'monster' movies: *Jaws* (1975) and *Jurassic Park* (1993). Many would agree that these are not merely blockbusters, but *serious* blockbusters. In other words, they are key examples of what has come to define the modern blockbuster movie. Both are basically genre films, meaning that they offer variations on established, popular formulae. They are both expensive productions that seek the widest possible audience: their aim is therefore to offer maximum entertainment through dramatic storytelling and spectacle. Both appeared during the summer, and as is now normal practice – since *Jaws* in fact – both were released simultaneously in large numbers of prints across cinemas with the aim of maximising profits.[4] It is this last part, of course, which really decides whether or not a film is a 'serious blockbuster'. In the case of *Jaws* and *Jurassic Park*, the box office, like their monster protagonists, was huge. Both films, in fact, broke box-office records at their time of release.

While few could deny that these were serious blockbusters, how many people would call them *serious films*? As popular cultural phenomena, we can't avoid them. But does this mean they are worthy of serious attention *in themselves*? By serious here, we mean it in its familiar sense of non-trivial ('thoughtful, earnest... responsible, not frivolous or reckless', again according to the OED). Exactly how a film can be serious is, I think, difficult to define – what is trivial for one person, for example, may be a serious subject for someone else – but the idea of seriousness in cinema is clearly reflected in the way different films are perceived and discussed. Films like *Jurassic Park* set out to entertain, and often succeed. As we'll see in this book, entertainment can itself be a serious business, requiring plenty of hard work, but this still involves them being set aside by critical opinion and classified as entertainment. 'Serious films' presumably look to do more than 'just entertain'; they seek to address a particular theme, historical moment or figure, or to say 'deeper' things about our world. A quick look at the kind of films that tend to win awards, and especially Academy Awards – biographical films, films about war or historical events, adaptations from literature – gives us an indication of how the film world has tended to separate entertainment and serious films.

Take 1993, for instance. The year Spielberg's dinosaur film roared onto our screens also saw the release of *Schindler's List*, Spielberg's film about the Holocaust. This film, not *Jurassic Park*, won a first Oscar for its director. *Schindler's List*, made for the same Hollywood studio as *Jurassic Park* (Universal), also happened to be fourth on the US box-office list that year. But because of its subject matter, we tend to think of *Schindler's List* as a serious film, not a blockbuster. Many might even consider the idea of a 'Holocaust blockbuster' an offensive one, or at least a contradiction in terms.

This last example indicates a basic divide in the way we often think about blockbusters. The blockbuster, this thinking suggests, can only deal with certain topics: other topics remain out of bounds, the domain of the serious film. It is quite reasonable that a fictional tale about cloned dinosaurs, and a real-life story about the attempted extermination of the Jewish people in Europe, demand different approaches and attitudes on the part of both film-maker and viewer. But does this mean that the blockbuster film that seeks its big summer audience need be 'just entertainment'? At some level, no film is ever *just* entertainment, just as no film is ever about nothing; not even *Jaws* and *Jurassic Park*, which in their own way deal with questions of politics and family, terror and peril. The quotations that began this introduction, however, go further, suggesting that the line dividing the serious and the trivial are blurred in the the third of the *Bourne* movies. A question we need to ask here, then, is this: do the kind of real-life issues identified in *The Bourne Ultimatum* find a natural home in the blockbuster action-thriller? Can a film labelled as a blockbuster, and described by one high-profile critic as 'a display of car-crashing, head-banging action mayhem'[5] really tackle serious issues? Does one thing get in the way of the other? And why, most importantly, do these questions matter?

They matter because the way things are labelled affects the way we think about them, and not always in a good way. In the case of *Ultimatum*, I will argue that we should take it seriously for the things it portrays. But I also think we should take it seriously for the *way* it portrays them. I mean here that our enjoyment of the film as a piece of 'car-crashing, head-banging action mayhem' need not be separated from its quality as a serious film: they are interconnected. It's clear from looking at reviews of the film, both from established journalists and casual bloggers, as well as the box-office figures, that it's a much-loved film. I love the film as a fan of the series, and as someone interested in blockbuster cinema in general. But it also engages me imaginatively and intellectually, as much as many other films not aimed at the blockbuster market. The point, though, is that movies, especially those that move as fast as *Ultimatum* does, can't do these things separately. They have to do them simultaneously.

This book will therefore question a basic assumption: that when we see a mainstream blockbuster movie we leave our brains at the popcorn stand. But I won't suggest that there are serious aspects of the film to look for *besides* its entertainment value, as this is no different to saying that blockbusters are fundamentally brainless, and only incidentally intelligent. I will suggest instead that we rethink what we are talking about when we use terms like 'blockbuster' and 'action film', or 'serious' and 'intelligent'. It's notable that in a year (2007) when the box office was dominated by other blockbuster sequels such as *Spider-Man 3* and *Shrek 2*, the major film prizes went to difficult, very non-generic Westerns: films like *There Will Be Blood*, or *No Country for Old Men*, which won the Best Picture Oscar at the 2008 ceremony. *Ultimatum* came away from those awards with three statuettes of its own, but all of them for the 'technical' awards – editing, sound, and sound editing. It didn't get a look-in for Best Picture, despite the fact that it got some of the best reviews of any film that year. Was this because, in the shorthand way most movies are pigeon-holed, it was an 'espionage movie', an 'action thriller', or 'just a blockbuster'? I think maybe it was, and I think we should question why this should be so.

Identifying The Bourne Ultimatum

What kind of film, then, is *The Bourne Ultimatum*? As I've suggested so far, identity is the real issue; a case of working out what sort of movie we are really dealing with. An idea which, conveniently, brings us round to the series' main question: who is Jason Bourne? Before we go any further, let's remind ourselves.

Jason Bourne, covert operative for the CIA – the USA's Central Intelligence Agency – is an amnesiac assassin running largely on instinct and his body's physical memory. He is also a man on a mission. When we first meet him, at the beginning of *The Bourne Identity*, he is being fished out of the Mediterranean. His rescuers think he is dead, and in some ways he is: a blank, a man with no name, no past, and – if his pursuers get to him first – no future. It turns out, as seen through a flashback in the first film, that Bourne the assassin had a moment of clarity mid-kill, and a dramatic change of heart: this explains how he came to be in the sea, half-dead with three bullets in his back. Now he wants out, but to his bosses back at the CIA, and in particular at 'Treadstone' – the training programme for state-sanctioned killers – his freedom is a threat. From the off, then, the storytelling dynamic of the series is a simple one: Bourne needs to find out who he is; at the same time, he is being hunted by those who know the truth and want to hide it. The end of the quest will see the truth revealed to him, but it will also bring him face to face with his enemies.

The three films, building up to the New York climax in *Ultimatum*, carry both Bourne and the viewer on a trail of snatched clues and uncovered evidence, as we try to work out who turned Bourne into a killer, and why. On the way, near the beginning of *Supremacy*, Bourne loses the girl he has found and loved (Marie, killed by an assassin's bullet intended for him). As well as setting Bourne back on the run once more, this time for revenge as well as answers, the second film sees Bourne forced to face up to past actions: actions that made him who he is, but also, possibly, made him want to forget. *Supremacy* therefore sends him to Berlin, and the scene of the crime: a mother and father gunned down by Bourne in front of their young daughter. After seeking out the now grown-up girl in Moscow at the end of the second film – not to erase evidence, but to reveal the truth and ask for forgiveness – the third film finds Bourne back on the trail of Treadstone, and now 'Blackbriar', the Treadstone upgrade of which he believes himself to be a subject.

The films are based on the trilogy of best-selling novels by Robert Ludlum, a writer who specialises in action-packed, information-dense spy thrillers with enigmatic three-word titles (*The Aquitaine Progression*, *The Matarese Countdown*, *The Scarlatti Inheritance*, to name just three). Unlike more recent adaptations of literary blockbusters, such as the Harry Potter films, the *Bourne* series was made some years after the books were published (Identity was published in 1980; the sequels, respectively, in 1986 and 1990). What's more, while the action of the first film (for its first hour at least) stays reasonably close to the novel, *Supremacy* and *Ultimatum* depart quite radically from their sources (no one knows what the 'ultimatum' in the third film really is, though I'm not sure it matters much).

Whether or not the films stick closely to the original plots, they are a great example of stripping a literary narrative down to its bare bones (all the novels are around 500 pages long, while the movies all come in at under two hours). Ludlum's novels lend themselves to filming not because of their dialogue (there's far too much of that), but because they are about information, and in particular the use of action and observation to get it: stuff that is much better on screen, which is all about seeing, showing and doing. Bourne's amnesia, in effect, makes him a kind of detective. For the most part, in detective narratives we see things through the detective's eyes – what literary and film theory call 'restricted' narration – sharing in his confusion and discoveries. This process becomes the story, the object of fascination for both protagonist and reader.[6] What gives this mystery an edge, and what makes it a thriller, is when we are also offered 'unrestricted' narration: vital information, for example, that the protagonist needs to know but doesn't, or knowledge of impending threat. In *Ultimatum*, the action is poised between restricted narration, as we follow Bourne in his frantic movement from city to city, and unrestricted narration, as we watch the CIA chiefs in New York tracking Bourne and planning his demise. In its movement back-and-forth, building up to the climax in Manhattan, the film demands that we keep up. If we miss a clue we might lose the plot; but then, if Bourne misses a clue, he may lose his life. Such are the stakes in this film.

Because the hunter is also the hunted, *Ultimatum* is also a race against time. It's a familiar type of story: the kind of narrative made popular by television shows such as *24* (Fox Television, 2001–2010), which is all about covering ground against the ticking of the clock. The relentless pace and split-second decision-making evoked in the film, together with the idea of battling against resilient enemies, is also something many of us experience through playing videogames (a game based loosely on the first film, *Robert Ludlum's The Bourne Conspiracy*, was actually produced by Sierra Entertainment and released in 2008; Electronic Arts also planned to develop a series of games based on the *Bourne* franchise, though these projects have not come to light). The idea of the protagonist as both hunter and hunted is also central to other recent action-thriller films: think of Steven Spielberg's *Minority Report* (2002) (where, in a twist on the classic detective genre, Tom Cruise has to solve the murder he is going to commit in the future), or the South Korean film *Oldboy* (2003), in which a man imprisoned without explanation for fifteen years is released and given five days to find out why. The *Bourne* series also has precedents in what I call 'running man' thrillers: a type of film made popular by Alfred Hitchcock's tales of innocent men being hunted by unknown pursuers over unknown crimes – films such as *The 39 Steps* (1935) and *North by Northwest* (1959). A more recent example of the genre would be the Harrison Ford vehicle *The Fugitive* (1993), in which a man, pursued by the FBI, tries to get to Chicago to reveal the truth of his wife's murder – a crime for which, again, he has been wrongly accused.

The last three films mentioned above also share some thematic elements with the *Bourne* films: the idea that the quest for survival or proof of innocence is also a quest for an important truth. This might be the presence in Britain of enemy spies (*The 39 Steps*) or the cover-up of faulty medical supplies for profit (*The Fugitive*). One thing we will need to consider is whether *Ultimatum*'s generic elements and its status as an action-espionage-thriller actually lend themselves to the kind of issues the film wants to explore. As we'll consider later, one of the ideas in the film is that the secret being tracked down by Bourne is so secret that *nobody knows about it*. As we see from the description of the film by John Patterson that opened this chapter, *The Bourne Ultimatum* brings to mind those aspects of international politics and security that are often not covered by news media. But then, the whole point about such 'black operations' as torture and assassination is that they tend to be covert; that is, covered up. It's for this reason that *Ultimatum* is most closely connected to the traditions of the 'conspiracy film': a genre best associated with certain American films of the 1970s – *The Parallax View* (1974), *Three Days of the Condor* (1975) and *All the President's Men* (1976), to take three prominent examples.[7]

The thematic and stylistic link to these films is not coincidental. Commentators on American cinema of the 1970s have shown how the disenchantment at the heart of conspiracy movies – the idea that the workings of government and society in general are so corrupt as to remain hidden from public view – responds to a crisis of belief in the system on the part of the political left: as one account puts it, these films 'reverse the polarities of earlier political thrillers, which generally affirmed American institutions, by suggesting that the source of evil was these very institutions'.[8] In taking those earlier films as a model, the point that *Ultimatum* wants to make is that the political climate of the mid-1970s is not so different from that of the mid-2000s. The 1970s films had as their backdrop an increasingly unpopular war in Vietnam, along with investigations into the legality and ethics of CIA operations, and the crisis of government represented by the 'Watergate' scandal (which I will discuss at more length in Chapter Two); behind the *Bourne* film series, though with implications in Britain as well as in the US, is another increasingly unpopular war (Afghanistan/Iraq), and concerns as to the legality and ethics of government actions (the justifications for invading Iraq, the policies behind the 'War on Terror', and the treatment of political prisoners in places such as Guantánamo Bay).

Given these consistencies between the two periods, the choice of director for *Ultimatum* also turns out to be a very specific one. As Patterson suggests in his interview with Paul Greengrass, the English-born director of both *Ultimatum* and *Supremacy* was not the obvious candidate to helm two parts of an action-thriller franchise (the first film was directed by Doug Liman, known more recently for the films *Mr. and Mrs. Smith* (2005) and *Jumper* (2008). Like many British directors working in Hollywood, Greengrass did not serve a typical Hollywood apprenticeship, having gone on after university to work on an influential investigative news show for Britain's ITV – *World in Action* (Granada, 1963–1998) – followed by a career making documentary films. It was this training that, as we shall see, informs the style of his *Bourne* sequels and other feature films; one that takes a documentary-like approach to filming fictional action. What eventually opened the door to *Bourne* was his film *Bloody Sunday* (2002), a 'docudrama' set on January 30 1972, about the killing by British soldiers of 14 demonstrators in the Northern Irish city of Derry. Originally intended just for television, the film ended up getting a theatrical release in the US, providing a showcase for Greengrass's idiosyncratic blend of politics and action, and helping him land *Supremacy*'s director's chair.

The issue of how a film can be both political and action-packed is one that interests Patterson, who concludes that 'the move from *Bloody Sunday* to Jason Bourne is an entirely natural and seamless one'.[9] From reading his comments, however, you get the feeling he is not quite sure about the political-action mix. As he writes: 'Despite its obvious appeal as a full-throttle action movie, *The Bourne Ultimatum* … has plenty in common with Greengrass's more obviously political movies'. Later, he suggests that the political meat of the movie is 'subtly embedded within a framework of thrills and violence, but it's there nonetheless'. Patterson is sympathetic to the idea of a political film involving action, but we should note the use here of 'despite' and 'but': it's a good example of the entertainment/serious split I talked about before. It's okay to combine Hollywood action and politics, this seems to say; only remember they are two different things, and one has nothing to do with the other. What, though, if we change 'despite' to 'because of'? Can the action movie be political in itself, *because* of what it is, rather than *despite* it?

In this regard, the general reception of *Ultimatum* by film critics makes interesting reading. The film's qualities as an action thriller are frequently praised, but often in a way that is double-edged. *Sight & Sound*, which in terms of British film magazines is at the more serious end of the spectrum, argues that the film 'completes a trilogy of the most exciting espionage thrillers ever made in Hollywood'.[10] *Sight & Sound* is published by the British Film Institute, and unlike most movie magazines (such as *Empire*), it is not market-driven in its choice of focus, tending to shy away from big-budget blockbusters. It's therefore interesting when voices as diverse as *Sight & Sound* and *Empire* agree on the same films. In the US, meanwhile, *The New Yorker* magazine recommended the film, but only as a 'genre' film: 'The material is formulaic, but, of all the current action franchises, this one is the most enjoyable'.[11] Similarly, Peter Bradshaw in the *Guardian* enjoyed the film, saying that it 'delivers a lot more entertainment bangs for your buck than any other action picture', though he also suggests that it is 'relentlessly ridiculous'.[12]

As a Hollywood product, expensively made and heavily marketed, the film can be appraised on a level with those other action films that were its summer rivals (alongside *Spider-Man 3* that year was *Die Hard 4.0* and the first *Transformers* film). Blockbuster films like these, the staple of Hollywood practice since the 1970s and the success of *Jaws* and *Star Wars* (1977), are seen by some as the embodiment of cinematic evil. For critics of these movies, they are money-making machines that bombard us first through marketing, and then bombard us again with big, brash and increasingly loud production values. And of all blockbusters, it's the action genre that comes in for the most critical scorn. 'The action film has become the emblem of what Hollywood does worst', writes David Bordwell, possibly America's best film historian.[13] Manohla Dargis, reviewing *Ultimatum* in the *New York Times*, agrees: 'It's easy to make people watch — just blow up a car, slit someone's throat'.[14] Looked at in this way, action is the easiest thing in the world to put on screen. What is there in the end to take seriously?

For one thing, we should take seriously the fact that people – a *lot* of people – like action films. It's important to understand why, as well as understanding why some action films are more popular than others. Also, if some action movies *are* lazy and dumb, not all of them are. Nor do they ever just blow up cars in order to get your attention (Bordwell thinks this too, and I'll be using some of his ideas in a later chapter). As I've said, though, I think we can go even further. Action thrillers can use the genre in a way that addresses political themes, but the political thrust is not separate from the action. *Ultimatum*, I'll argue, engages with serious ideas, as well as the mind, as it entertains; or rather, it entertains *by* engaging the mind. This, in the end, is why I think we should regard the film as a serious blockbuster: it engages the mind first and foremost *by entertaining*.

Footnotes

1. John Patterson, 'Killer Instinct', *Guardian*, 6 August 2007.

2. James Dyer, Review of *The Bourne Ultimatum*, *Empire* Online, August 2007.

3. Richard Maltby, *Hollywood Cinema*, second edition (Malden, Oxford, Melbourne and Berlin: Blackwell, 2003), p. 160.

4. See Warren Buckland, *Directed by Steven Spielberg* (New York and London: Continuum, 2006).

5. Peter Bradshaw, review of *The Bourne Ultimatum*, *Guardian*, 17 August 2007.

6. See David Bordwell, *Narrative in the Fiction Film* (London: Methuen, 1985), pp. 64–70.

7. To emphasise the similarities, *The Parallax View* is about a secret society that recruits political assassins; while *Three Days of the Condor* involves a covert CIA plot to control Middle-Eastern oil reserves.

8. Michael Ryan and Douglas Kellner, *Camera Politica: The Politics and Ideology of Contemporary American Film* (Bloomington and Indianapolis: Indiana University Press, 1988), p. 95.

9. Patterson, 'Killer Instinct'.

10. Demetrios Matheou, review of *The Bourne Ultimatum*, *Sight & Sound*, 17.10 (2007), 50–51 (50).

11. David Denby, 'War Wounds', *The New Yorker*, 6 August 2007.

12. Bradshaw, op cit.

13. David Bordwell, *The Way Hollywood Tells It: Story and Style in Modern Movies* (Berkeley: University of California Press, 2006), p. 104.

14. Manohla Dargis, review of *The Bourne Ultimatum*, *New York Times*, 3 August 2007.

Summary and questions

- The way certain films are labelled makes a difference to the way they are discussed. Certain film genres (for example, the action film) and film industries (for example, Hollywood) tend to be associated with 'blockbuster' cinema. These are often contrasted with other films considered to be 'serious' films or 'artistic' films.

- The different labels given to films affects the way they are received and discussed, whether by professional critics, or by the industry itself, in the case of awards.

- The blockbuster's association with entertainment and economics means it is often assumed to be a more trivial, less serious kind of film-making.

- Is *The Bourne Ultimatum* an obvious 'blockbuster' movie?

- Do you think that the distinction between 'serious' and 'entertainment' cinema is a false one?

- Why do you think blockbuster cinema is often termed 'popcorn' cinema? What does this kind of naming suggest about attitudes towards it?

- Is it possible for blockbuster films to engage seriously with real-world issues?

Chapter Two: 'My argument is not with you' – The Politics of *Bourne*

At the end of *The Bourne Supremacy*, after completing his personal mission in Moscow, we see Jason Bourne in New York. In a room high up somewhere in the city, Bourne surveys the CIA office building opposite. His words to Pamela Landy on the phone alert her to Bourne's presence, and her recognition that she is being watched: Bourne disappears into the streets, and the second film ends. As we know, and as we'll discuss later, this scene reoccurs in *Ultimatum*, but not until over an hour in. Its place at the end of the second film, then, seems designed to bring the overall narrative trajectory of the series into focus. Whatever has just taken place in Moscow and Berlin, it suggests, was just part of the battle: the real target lies in America, and the source of Bourne's predicament.

In the opening sequence of *Ultimatum*, meanwhile, an injured Bourne is fleeing from a police pursuit in what a subtitle identifies as Moscow. No opening credits, establishing shots or recapping flashbacks delay the action: as happens frequently in this film, we are hurled into the middle of things without explanation. Anyone familiar with the previous film may guess by now that the New York scene was a flash-forward, and that we have jumped back to where we had previously left off. If we remember, Bourne's efforts to reach the teenage girl in Moscow involved him negotiating the efforts of Kirill to dispose of him – Kirill being the Russian agent whose earlier attempt on Bourne's life resulted in the death of Marie. This finished up, as tends to be the case in the last two *Bourne* films, in an almighty pile-up that left Kirill half-dead and from which Bourne, also carrying a gunshot wound, limped away.

Back to the third film, and we hear a Russian voice on the police radio confirming Bourne as a suspect in the car chase and crash. Besides these voices, there is no dialogue; merely the noises of trains and cars that surround Bourne's flight towards an unattended pharmacy, followed by the crash of medicine bottles and the ripping of syringe packs as he looks to treat his wounds. Two cautious policemen enter. The first one is taken down and disarmed by the American, who points the gun at the remaining Russian. The policeman begs him not to shoot. 'My argument is not with you', Bourne replies in the policeman's native tongue. He then departs, after which the film's title finally appears on the screen.

Starting a film this way can be risky, but I believe it works in this case. This sequence doesn't provide much information, either in terms of what has gone before, or what is going to happen next. It leaves no space and time for the viewer to settle in, but rather throws them into the action: catch up and get clued up quickly, the film seems to say; something it will keep on saying for its 115 minute duration. This kind of approach, which avoids the neat sort of presentation and convention we often find at the beginning of movies, succeeds in hiding its status as a movie: we are instead pitched into a world in motion, with its own apparent life and dynamic beyond the time and space of the film itself. This is also the third part in a series, of course, and many viewers will not need any establishing information. But while the film starts at pace, there is little in this opening sequence that is vital to the action of the third film; in this way, anyone joining the series at number three will not be totally thrown.

J.B., or not J.B.?

Aside from bridging the space and time between *Supremacy* and *Ultimatum*, this opening sequence also reminds us where the films stand politically. When Bourne says that his argument is not with the Russians, this is a pointed reminder of the political climate of the *Bourne* films, and the climate of the twenty-first century more generally. Genre films such as the thriller, especially in the way they use espionage, political conspiracies and terrorism as the source of their plots, tend at some level to reflect the times in which they were made. So it is that films like *The 39 Steps* have pre-echoes of the emerging Nazi threat, while *North by Northwest*'s debonair European villain is vaguely connected to some communist-led deception. Film critic Philip French suggests that the *Bourne* films look back to Cold War espionage novels such as John le Carré's *The Spy Who Came in From the Cold* (1963) and Len Deighton's *The Ipcress File* (1962), both of which became popular films.[15] Jason Bourne's most obvious reference point, of course, is that other J.B. – James Bond, whose globetrotting career as a British secret agent, in Ian Fleming's original novels and in more than twenty films, has seen him grapple with just about every so-called security threat, and every ethnic and cultural stereotype, for over fifty years. Since the fall of the Berlin Wall in 1989, however, and the demise of the Soviet Union that came in its wake – and with it the end of the Cold War – the politics of the spy thriller have been obliged to change.

If the *Bourne* franchise is conscious of having Bond as a predecessor, *Ultimatum*'s prologue seems a conscious attempt to reference the Bond films' famous pre-credit scenes. But Bourne does not escape in spectacular fashion here; he looks terrible, can barely run, and doesn't have a speedboat or parachute, let alone a place to use them. There is no clever payoff line (in English) at a temporary (foreign) villain's expense, as we often see in the Bond films. The pre-credit sequences in the Bond series are designed to illustrate both how accomplished and smooth the hero is, but also how accomplished and smooth the film itself is: hence the tendency to begin with spectacular stunts or flash gadgets. *Ultimatum*, on the other hand, looks determined both to show a vulnerable, wounded hero, and a very un-flashy kind of cinematic style. Above all, there is no stylish framing of the hero, as in the iconic 'gun-barrel shot' of 007 that the films usually open with. The first of the Daniel Craig Bonds, *Casino Royale* (2006), is widely considered to be a 'reboot' of the franchise (I discuss this in Chapter Eight): as such, it opted for a black-and-white, back-to-basics flashback for its pre-credit scene, the narrative function of which was to show how Bond murderously attained his '00' status. But even with this, the film could not resist inserting its most famous image.

By referencing Bond in such a contrasting way, *Ultimatum*'s point is not so much that cinematic fashions have changed, but that the world has changed, and with it, there is a need for new ways to represent it. The world of Bourne is above all one in which not just the Berlin Wall has collapsed, but with it the borders that defined 'good' from 'bad', and even 'them' from 'us'. The array of assassins sent after him are marked by name as non-American – in *Ultimatum* they are called Desh and Paz – but Bourne's argument is not with them, but with the masters who dispatched them: Noah Vosen, the head of Blackbriar who orders Bourne's death from the CIA hub, and Ezra Kramer, the CIA chief. The *Bourne* series is, from the start, not about Them and Us, but about how We are already both Them and Us.

Secrets and lies

The decision in *Ultimatum* to use a journalist as the information link between Blackbriar and Bourne is a key one in terms of the film's politics, as it puts into focus the potential limits to knowledge on the part of our news media. We first see Simon Ross, security correspondent with the UK's *Guardian* newspaper, meeting a man – CIA station chief Neal Daniels – in a restaurant in Turin. Ross is on the trail of Bourne and Blackbriar, piecing together the fragmented traces of information left in Bourne's wake. 'What joins the dots?' he asks his source. Notice how this scene is filmed: in long shot, picking out the two men's conversation as if observed from a distance (Fig2), then in tight over-the-shoulder shots which reveal nothing but Daniels' anxious face (Fig 3). This approach, used frequently for close dialogue sequences in the film, fits the context: this is a conversation that should not be taking place (Daniels, we note, tells Ross to turn off his tape recorder), and one which will ultimately cost both men their lives. Ross does not work this out until it is too late, but his anxious glances on his return to England suggest the gravity of this newly acquired knowledge.

Fig 2: 'Observed' meetings

Fig 3: Telling secrets

Greengrass, in the audio commentary to the *Ultimatum* DVD, has said that he wanted to bring to the film the mood of those conspiracy movies I mentioned previously; in particular *All the President's Men*, a film about the Watergate scandal that rocked the American political system, and which led to the resignation of President Richard Nixon in 1974. The seriousness of Watergate, which centred on the apparent use of Republican Party money to fund the robbery of Democratic Party offices (by ex-CIA men, as it happens), was that it brought to light the hidden workings of political forces. In this case, the trail led back to the President himself, who is believed to have played a role in covering up the affair: such findings cast doubts over the trustworthiness of leaders in general. Such a scandal could only reinforce the unease of a country whose previous decade had experienced the trauma of a long and fruitless war in Vietnam, and a series of political assassinations. It was during this period that the role and power of the CIA were called into question; the backdrop against which the *Bourne* novels were originally written: but how much of a comparison did the film's director, along with his screenwriters (Tony Gilroy, Scott Burns and George Nolfi), wish to make between the 1970s and 2007? And where are the differences?

In *All the President's Men* the heroes who break the Watergate story are two journalists from the Washington Post, Bob Woodward and Carl Bernstein, on whose actual book the film is based (they are played in the movie by Robert Redford and Dustin Hoffman, two of the biggest movie stars of the time). If the film is paranoid about American politics, it shows a faith at least in the value of investigative journalism, and the ability of news media to reveal the truth. *Ultimatum*'s Simon Ross, by contrast, may have good intentions, but he can never be the hero of this film: the stakes, it seems, are just too high. 'This isn't some story in a newspaper', Bourne tells him later in Waterloo station, minutes before a Blackbriar assassin puts a bullet through Ross's head: 'This is real'. There is an obvious irony intended here: it is supposed to be the news media that show us real life, not the movies. Maybe the point here, which is also one about the value of fiction to suggest facts, is that movies can tell us what they want, whereas news media, arguably, can only tell us so much. At some level the covert workings of governments and intelligence services cannot be told: this, after all, is why they're called covert. Ross's purpose, then, is to be what Greengrass calls 'the innocent man in the middle': the unfortunate messenger that leads Bourne to Daniels, and eventually to Blackbriar.

This is a world, then, where security forces become agents of terror in the name of security itself. As a key feature of *Ultimatum*, much of which operates through the cross-cutting, cat-and-mouse game between Bourne on the street and Noah Vosen's anti-terrorist hub, the film can be located within a line of American cinema made in the wake of the 11 September 2001 ('9/11') attacks on New York's World Trade Center and the Pentagon building in Washington. While the film never openly references the attacks, there are subtle hints towards the climate of modern Western life in the aftermath of 9/11, as well as the subsequent bombings in Madrid and London in 2004 and 2005 (both cities feature in the third instalment). One of the major post-9/11 transformations in both the US and UK, under the closely-allied Bush and Blair governments, was the stepping up of security intelligence and the implications of this for foreign policy – culminating in 2003 with the invasion of Iraq and subsequent war. In America, in 2002, we saw the birth of a new department: Homeland Security. Yet 'homeland security', Greengrass's film suggests, comes not just at the price of intervention overseas, but of threats to our everyday freedoms. Ross is first identified as a security risk because of a casually spoken word: more specifically, because of his reference to Blackbriar in a phone call made to his editor, just as he returns to Heathrow from his Turin meeting. In a fluid cut from British MI5 offices to the CIA hub, via two computer screens, we see the word intercepted and relayed between intelligence agencies across the globe (Figs 4 and 5). This is a real-life keyword identification programme, called Echelon (you hear it mentioned in the dialogue if you listen closely). James Bond and his pal Q could only dream of such stuff when the original Bond novels were being written. If we believe such things are used in this way – Echelon is real after all, not the invention of fiction – then it makes old-fashioned spy work seem redundant, as well as reminding us that counter-terrorist intelligence can be used not only for our benefit, but against us.

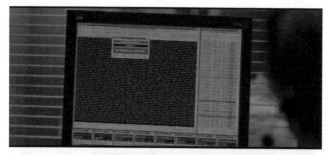

Fig 4: Keyword identi- fication relayed from London...

Fig 5: to New York.

There is one more J.B. we need to mention: Jack Bauer (what is it with those initials?), Counter Terrorist agent extraordinaire. Bauer is usually quite at home with such technology. Or at least his team back at the Counter Terrorist Unit are, with their cool banks of computer terminals and head-microphones, feeding vital split-screen information to Jack as he strives each season to redeem himself and save America. For anyone who isn't up to speed here, this J.B. is the protagonist of the TV show *24*, the insomniac to Bourne's amnesiac. The similarities between Bourne and Bauer, who first appeared on American television at the end of 2001, are numerous: both men are products of US intelligence agencies; both are highly-trained, multi-skilled and seemingly indestructible; both are buff and blond with a fondness for wearing black. What's more, both Bauer and the cinematic Bourne were created before 9/11, but first appeared on-screen after it: both have consequently been seen in relation to the events, and indeed have grown up largely defined by them.

The key difference between Bourne and Bauer is that, even if Bauer frequently goes rogue, he is at heart a loyal servant to the President, and a protector of US interests. There are many reasons for *24*'s popularity, first among which is that it is very well put together, with enough narrative hooks to make the viewer forget either the dubious politics or clichéd characters. If rolling with Bauer as the clock ticks involves a slightly guilty sense of fun at times (he is particularly fond of torture, after all), enemies of the state, especially in the early seasons, are mostly clear cut: they are non-Americans, or in the case of those insider terrorists within government or CTU itself, un-American Americans tainted by shady foreign influence. Bourne's patriotism, I will suggest at a later point, barely comes into play until the very end of *Ultimatum*. His loyalty is principally to himself, partly because he can't remember anyone, but also because he has a ruthless streak. Bourne's distrust is not based on what the authorities tell him: how could it be, if they are the ones who want him dead?

Homeland (In)Security

The fact that *Ultimatum* continually positions a high-tech anti-terrorist computer hub against Bourne, rather than as the back-up that supports him, is the main indication of where the film stands in relation to *24*, and in turn the ethos of Homeland Security. *24*, during the George Bush years at least, is generally on-message as far as foreign policy is concerned (Fox Television, the company that produces the show, also produces America's most unapologetically right-wing news programming). *Ultimatum* appears to reject the message endorsed by *24*. Vosen in particular – 'It ends when we've won', he says at one point – becomes a kind of mouthpiece for the outgoing Bush administration, whose 'War on Terror', and with it the dragged-out conflicts in Iraq and Afghanistan, are its main legacy. For Vosen, 'just cause' and 'international law' are outdated concepts thrown out in the service of victory; just as for George Bush, some might say, UN resolutions and votes were seen as the ineffectual and irrelevant acts of a debating society.

If we look at Greengrass's other work, we can further understand and put into context *Ultimatum*'s politics. Greengrass is outspokenly left-wing in his political views, and has openly worked in opposition to governments, even in defiance of them. Greengrass had some previous involvement with espionage before Bourne, as the co-author of *Spycatcher*, a 1985 book by former MI5 officer Peter Wright, which was so frank in its description of British secret service operations that the Conservative government of the day tried to ban it. *Bloody Sunday*, mentioned earlier, aroused controversy for its representation of British paratroopers, and their supposed responsibility for the killings that took place on the day in question. Between his two *Bourne* movies, meanwhile, Greengrass made *United 93* (2006). The film imaginatively recounts, in real time, the flight of the titular United Airlines airliner on the day of the 9/11 attacks: the so-called 'fourth plane', headed for the White House, but which possibly as a consequence of passenger action, came down short of its target in a Pennsylvania field. We can only speculate what really happened on board Flight 93 – there were no survivors – though immediately after the events, this 'prevented' terrorist strike at the symbolic heart of America took on its own symbolic resonance: one of patriotic martyrdom. Greengrass's film, however, offers a more pragmatic and less mythologising reading of events, suggesting that the passengers' attempts to storm the cockpit was from honest self-preservation, aiming to disable the hijackers and land the plane. The film therefore goes against the grain of some other post-9/11 representations, in the way it 'promotes official incompetence over conspiracy, eschews nationalist appeal, and shows the hijackers – as well as the passengers – addressing their God'.[16] Controversial as this might be, we can see it as an honest attempt to wrestle back individual lives from their fate as political pawns; as well as an effort to dig a little deeper, to explore the causes behind events and not just their effects.

We'll come back to many of these issues at later points. The ideas outlined in this chapter have been intended to show, in an introductory way, how the choices made in film or television narratives are always political in some respect. Even when the material is 'just' an action thriller, or 'just' a TV show, the way things are shown, along with the way some things are *not* shown, are part of the way movies and shows create their particular world. Even if we choose not to take them too seriously, it's important to understand how much representations in film and television have contributed to the way we see the world, and how they are influential maybe *because* we don't take them so seriously. Above all, it's important to see how the kind of distinctions and dialogue set up between the *Bourne* series and other cultural texts show us that no representation in film and television is 'normal' or 'natural': there are always choices being made, and agendas being set. *The Bourne Ultimatum* takes this idea to extremes. As we'll see in the next chapter, it suggests a world in which nothing we see can be really trusted, or at least clearly read: at some points, it suggests, not even the film itself.

Footnotes

15. Philip French, review of *The Bourne Ultimatum*, *Observer*, 19 August 2007. The film versions of *The Spy Who Came in From the Cold* and *The Ipcress File* were both produced in 1965.

16. J. Hoberman, 'Unquiet Americans', *Sight & Sound*, 16.10 (2006), 20–23 (22).

Summary and questions

- While similar in many ways, *The Bourne Ultimatum* establishes essential differences between itself and other similar films and television shows, such as the James Bond series or *24*.

- The references in the *Bourne* series indicate the global political contexts in which the films are situated. We can also read *Ultimatum* in the light of other films by its director, Paul Greengrass.

- The film's emphasis on news media, and this media's inability to fully comprehend the world, situates *Ultimatum* within the tradition of 'conspiracy' movies.

- Is it possible for a film to communicate what our news media cannot? Are there any reasons why we should trust fiction films over television news and newspapers?

- The choice of what to show in a film, and what not to show, is ultimately the choice of the film-makers. To what extent does this make all films 'political' films?

Chapter Three: Jason Bourne at the Battle of Waterloo – The Style of *Bourne*

Suddenly they all took off at a gallop. A few minutes later Fabrice saw, twenty paces ahead, a ploughed field whose surface seemed to be moving in an odd manner ... He heard a sharp cry beside him: two hussars were falling, hit by shot; and, as he looked at them, they were already twenty paces behind the escort ...

Ah! So now at last I'm under fire! He thought ... He could see white smoke of the battery a distance away and, amid the regular, continuous booming produced by the cannonade, he thought he could make out some volleys that were much closer; he could not begin to understand what was going on.[17]

The excerpt above, in its original French, was written in 1839. Stendhal – the pen name of novelist Henri Beyle – wanted to capture the feelings of disorientation and chaos that characterise the experience of war: in this particular case, the Battle of Waterloo, between the armies of Napoleon and Wellington, which took place in Belgium in 1815. Few of us reading this book, probably, will get to experience the fear and confusion of ground warfare. Yet that doesn't stop wars going on, and since Stendhal's day, the sights, sounds and shocks of war have been a constant feature in many books, films and television shows.

This part of Stendhal's novel, *The Charterhouse of Parma*, is famous because it attempts to place the reader alongside, or even in the mind of, its protagonist (in this case, a young Italian called Fabrice). Here, as in any narrative art form, the details observed and the perspective from which this description is given are choices made by the writer. We can get an idea of what this means if we think about the different ways the battle might have been portrayed. We might have seen it from the point of view of two opposing soldiers, rather than just one. We might have seen it from the generals' view somewhere up on a hill, overlooking the battle like some kind of board game (Leo Tolstoy does this a bit with Napoleon in his novel *War and Peace* [1865–69]). Alternatively, the whole thing could be reported, as it might be in old history books, as a series of statistics; a record of men and ground gained and lost. Stendhal chose to do it his way partly because he'd been to war himself, having served in the Napoleonic army during their retreat from Moscow in 1812. But mainly, he chose this style because it fitted the story and its main protagonist; a naive teenager giddy with thoughts of being a soldier, but with no idea how to get to the front.

Skip forward a couple of centuries. Simon Ross, *Guardian* correspondent, receives a phone call in his newspaper's main office. A no-nonsense American voice at the other end of the line tells him to get to Waterloo Station, south entrance, by 12.30. 'Who is this?' asks Ross (like any decent journalist, Ross asks a lot of questions). He takes a taxi to the appointed place and receives another phone call. He turns to his left to retrieve his mobile phone before realising that the ring tone is coming from his right side: another phone has been placed into his jacket pocket. Again, the questions ('*What the hell is going on?*'); in answer, only instructions. Ross's attention, and with it our own, is drawn towards a series of otherwise innocent-looking things: a car parked across the road; a man in a building opposite; a group of people at a bus stop. As if taking up Ross's point of view, the camera pans round with a blur to locate its object, or makes sudden lurches into focus with the zoom lens. The voice on Ross's phone keeps talking, amplified on the soundtrack for our benefit: keep watching, keep moving, do what I say. Ross leaves the bus stop as a red double-decker passes. A man and a woman rush out of a car and onto the bus. Almost too quickly to register, a boy in a hooded top is injected in the neck and dragged off before screaming passengers. The journalist keeps moving, looking anxiously behind him, that practice look he tried out at Heathrow now replaced by the real thing. He stops finally at a covered entrance linking the street with the main station concourse. A man he's never seen before, but whose voice he will recognise, walks rapidly toward him. No time for niceties: 'Who's your source?' the man asks. Ross answers with another question, the slightly peeved look now one of full-on panic: '*What's going on?*'

What's going on – though there's no need for Bourne to say it – is that right now, Waterloo station is a war zone. And whether he likes it or not, Simon Ross just became a soldier.

Holding up the mirror

These two Waterloo scenes, separated by two centuries, are both attempts to evoke the world as experienced by their protagonists, with all the confusion and terror that comes with it. This aim to represent in art a sense of what the world is like, and to make it believable for readers and viewers, is the oldest practice in the Western tradition: so much so that for many people the ability to be 'realistic' or 'true to life' is the essential purpose of art itself. This process of trying to show the real world through art is often referred to as *mimesis*: a Greek word, first used in its critical sense by the philosopher Plato, which roughly translates as 'imitation', though more broadly describes 'the relationship between artistic images and reality: art [as] a copy of the real'.[18] Whether or not we use the term to describe something, all of us at some point make judgments based on mimesis: to call a film or television show 'believable' or 'realistic', or conversely to say 'that wouldn't happen' or 'it's not like that', is to interpret according to 'mimetic' values.[19]

The problem with mimesis, but also what makes it so interesting, is that there is no obvious way to define 'reality' to begin with, given that any number of people might see the same thing in any number of ways. Besides, if reality were so obvious, we would have no need for mimetic art. Hamlet, in Shakespeare's play of the same name, tells the visiting actors to 'hold ... the mirror up to nature' (Act 3, Scene 2); a concept refined by Stendhal (a big admirer of the English dramatist) when he describes art as 'a mirror journeying down the high road',[20] capable of reflecting both the blue sky above and the dirty puddles below. The problem with Hamlet's view is that it suggests nature is both easily observable and constant, which it isn't. For one thing, what one culture might have taken for granted (for example, that the Earth was the centre of the universe, a common notion in Shakespeare's time) would seem absurd in later eras. Stendhal's point, therefore, is that a realistic art has to be complex, and recognise the fact that a view of the world has to contain the viewpoint of the observer. With his would-be Napoleon, he wanted to capture this sense that warfare cannot be 'read' in a straightforward way. We see at once Fabrice's imagination at work, and also how this imagination is out of sync with the events around him: both the hero's delusions (the narrator's viewpoint), and his struggle to make sense of events around him (the hero's viewpoint), make up what is then recorded on the page. This in turn becomes itself a kind of realism, though an ironic one, that explores the gaps between individual perception and the wider world.

Ultimatum's Waterloo sequence asks similar questions: can reality be understood merely by looking? It may have been possible once – a lot of Renaissance painting, for example, is based around the idea that the world can be represented from an ideal, singular viewpoint – but only in terms of what people assumed reality to be. To compare a film like *Ultimatum* to the films of early cinema from one hundred years previously, is to be reminded that style in films is not just a question of fashion or choice; it reflects changing attitudes about how we see reality. If we look today at films from the early 1900s, it often seems as if reality was something out there waiting to be recorded: just put a camera there and roll the film. This is why it was quite popular in the first two decades of cinema to see films of 'foreign people', or what we call 'ethnographic' film. Interesting as these films often are, it is important to remember that they are based on an essential division of power: we watch and film, '*they*' get watched and filmed. The right to look and record, and the issue of whether we should be looked at, is not questioned. As for the early fiction film, these were often quite stiff, stagey affairs; a legacy of the idea that film was essentially recorded theatre, or a representation of the world as if from the perspective of an ideally placed viewer.[21]

As we've already seen, the world of *Ultimatum* is one in which people do not simply watch: they *get watched*. The film does something very significant in regard to this idea, turning it into a principle of style. We saw earlier with Ross, leaving the airport, that his anxious glances to the side seemed to look for a camera following him; just as his discussion with Daniels appeared to be observed, espionage fashion, by the same movie camera that films the scene. This is taken further in the Waterloo sequence and the action that precedes it. Note the way that a shot of an agent at the CIA hub reporting on Ross's movements cuts away to a high helicopter shot, showing a car – presumably Ross's taxi – passing over the Thames. We've seen shots like this hundreds of times, in all kinds of films, but something important happens in this instance: the camera zooms out to get a clearer shot of the car's destination. The film camera, then, actually becomes for a moment a helicopter surveillance camera tracking down its target: the same one used by the CIA agent. This is a very effective technique, as it confuses the barrier between the film's camera, which we generally are not made aware of (see below), and the surveillance camera in the action itself, which suddenly becomes present.

The majority of the film's action, as we know, consists of a back-and-forth movement between Bourne and the CIA hub. The fact that we see so much of the 'live' action relayed onto the screens in New York emphasises the way modern life is lived on camera; in this case, in the eye of surveillance. One of Greengrass's aims in making the film was to show the British capital in a less familiar light; one removed from either the glossy interiors and gadgetry of a Bond movie, or the postcard, festive London seen in a lot of British romantic comedy.[22] One of the ways the director achieved this was to film during the daytime in a busy working station, rather than recreate it after-hours with hundreds of extras. Matt Damon and a reduced camera and sound crew were therefore working quickly among actual commuters, often filming simultaneously from different angles: the film-making here replicating the multiple perspective of CCTV cameras. As the film's cinematographer Oliver Wood suggests, this process meant that the final images had a more spontaneous, almost accidental quality.[23] Filmed in this way, we see a London that is cold, crowded, and policed. Of course Bourne, always one step ahead, has chosen Waterloo for a reason: as we're reminded, it's the busiest station in London and therefore a surveillance nightmare for Vosen's team. Whether or not we buy into the idea that our every move and phone call is being monitored from afar, what isn't in doubt here are the tools of surveillance themselves: these are all too conspicuous in London (a city with one of the highest numbers of CCTV cameras in the world). The repeated shot of Bourne looking up to see a bank of cameras, followed by the return shot of them 'looking' at him (Fig 6 and 7), is so common in this sequence that the cameras are almost characters in themselves.

Fig 6: Bourne looks up at the CCTV cameras...

Fig 7: and the cameras 'look back at him'.

With Bourne using his skill and resources to outwit this photographic army, and in turn Vosen's efforts to capture or eliminate Ross, the sequence manages to blend entertainment and political content: by following the action here, we inevitably follow the logic and workings of a surveillance society. It was also this sequence that attracted most attention in reviews of the film. This is not surprising: it's one of the film's longest set-pieces of action (from Ross's arrival at the station, up to the end of the underground chase, the episode lasts just over ten minutes), but it is also the sequence which best shows off *Ultimatum*'s cinematic style. But how exactly do we define this style? I've suggested above that this Battle of Waterloo emphasises a dizzying sense of disorientation and tension, as well as communicating the idea that there are forces observing our every move. But for many viewers it is also totally exhilarating. How does it manage to do all these things at once?

Joining the dots: editing style

A main thing to focus on in the film is the way it's put together; in other words, how it's edited. Editing – in its simplest terms, the way a movie is assembled from the available filmed material – is fundamental to Hollywood cinema, often controversially so, though it is also for some viewers one of the least obvious aspects of a movie. This is not the fault of any particular viewer, but rather an effect of editing itself, as the aim of editing within Hollywood film traditions, like in most narrative films, is to make editing itself unnoticeable. Films achieve this by making the sense of space and time coherent and fluid within any sequence of action, even when the sequence is in reality made up of various fragments of film, possibly shot over the space of days or even weeks. Because this practice is designed to evoke a continuous temporal and spatial movement, historians of film call this 'continuity editing' or the 'continuity system'. It is this sense of a lifelike (or mimetic) time and space that helps us forget that, in actuality, we're not watching real life, but pieces of recorded action stuck together to *look like* real life.

Continuity editing is effective because it is a technique that stops us thinking about technique. If we look closely at a film, though, we can be surprised to find how frequently one shot of film gives way, or 'cuts', to another. In the heyday of the Hollywood studios, between 1930 and 1960, it was typical for the shot to change every 8 to 11 seconds on average (this measurement has come to be known as the Average Shot Length, or ASL).[24] Older films can feel harder to watch these days for many reasons, but one of them is the 'slow' speed of cutting compared to modern movies. In films from the 1930s and 1940s it's common to watch dialogue scenes in which two or more people are in shot, with the camera barely moving, for ten, twenty, or more seconds. This becomes less common after the 1940s, and is almost unheard of in recent decades. From the 1960s cutting became faster, and notably it was action films such as *Goldfinger* (1964) – with an ASL of 4 seconds – that revved up the editing pace.[25] The feeling of speed and dynamism that shorter shot lengths can bring about naturally lends itself to action films, so it is no surprise that, at the turn of the new century, the shortest ASLs are found in this genre: Michael Bay's *Armageddon* (1998) has an ASL of 2.3 seconds; the same director's *Bad Boys II* (2003) clocks in at under 2 seconds, as do other action or adventure movies such as *Lara Croft: Tomb Raider* (2001), *The Transporter* (2002) and *Pirates of the Caribbean* (2003).[26] The evidence of the early twenty-first century, as David Bordwell shows, is that films are getting faster and faster, with implications even for other film genres, such as comedy or historical dramas, which are following suit with more hectic cutting speeds.[27]

It is easy to see why a lot of film critics and also film-makers are worried about this tendency. Shorter shot lengths, the logic goes, implies shorter attention spans, and in turn the need to wrestle the viewer's attention with even quicker cutting. The lack of critical affection for the action/adventure movie may be due to the fact that it has become the main staple of popular film entertainment in recent years, epitomised by the various

Marvel and DC comic adaptations, or the *Transformers* series. For some, this relentless speeding-up is at the same time a kind of mental slowing-down. As Jonathan Romney writes in his review of *Ultimatum*, it is 'usually an article of faith ... that high-speed cutting, and the kind of cinema that thrives on it, doesn't let the viewer's mind function, just bludgeons it into a stupor'.[28] In other words, the shift from one shot to the next is so frenetic that the viewer has no time to see what's really going on; and as we know, if we don't know what's going on, there's no coherence and no story. The point that Romney wants to stress, though, is that *Ultimatum* is itself an example of modern high-speed cutting. Try watching the Waterloo sequence and count each cut between shots: you won't be able to without slowing the film down. In the ten-minute sequence there are, in fact, over three hundred and seventy cuts: an ASL of 1.6 seconds! This is not so much breathless as suffocating. What then, if anything, makes *Ultimatum* different from *Transformers*?

The point is that in *Ultimatum*, the choice of high-speed cutting is not just reflecting contemporary action-movie trends, but adds to the sense of paranoia and anxiety that the film wants to evoke. Less is not more in this case. Look again at Fig 6 and 7, and think about how this kind of film-making operates at speed. The protagonist looks up, drawing the viewer's attention to his eyeline. A following shot indicates the object of his look. Following this, the protagonist reacts according to what they have seen. Cinema as a narrative medium works around these kinds of codes: eyelines and directions of movement point the viewer toward new spaces of action, visual causes and effects that we are constantly anticipating and processing. One of the fun things about action cinema is to see the hero take in their surroundings, and then quickly make use of objects to hand: we as viewers can often take pleasure in anticipating the subsequent action. But equally, if the film surprises us with something unexpected, we enjoy the surprise. In a film looking for a greater sense of realism, though, time is of the essence. The action in *Ultimatum*, as the above example shows, happens much faster in actuality than on the page: Bourne doesn't have the luxury of time. In order for the viewer to feel this urgency, the shots do not rest on anything for long: they cannot, as another line of attack needs to be assessed and defended. Fast cutting is therefore a way of emphasising the stakes involved in split-second observation and decision.

It's also about power, as I've hinted above. Having time to observe and contemplate action is a sign of being in control. Think about the way James Bond often looks so cool and unhurried, choosing his next move like a golfer sizing up a shot. If Bond is golf, Bourne is ice-hockey: pass or get crashed, shoot or be slammed. It's almost impossible to stay up to speed in the Waterloo sequence. Whether it's the rapid movement of a camera or the sudden appearance of a suspicious figure, things are too fast for us to anticipate, and almost too fast to process. The idea is to keep you, like the protagonists, on your toes: rather than just bashing you over the head, the film, Romney suggests, 'prods your mind into a state of thrilled alertness'.[29] The nightmare it evokes is the one experienced by Ross: that of knowing something or someone is after you, but never quite knowing from where.

Of course we are not just watching Ross: we are watching Bourne, and more importantly watching *through* Bourne. Ross, along with Vosen and his assassin Paz, are the problem; Bourne is the solution. In this way *Ultimatum* is a good example of the importance of varied point of view in film. The action described above in reference to Figures 6 and 7 – the sequence of look, process, react – is repeated throughout the Waterloo episode. This helps to better orient the action for the viewer, showing us where we are, what's going on, cueing us to think ahead towards the piece of action that follows. Because Bourne shows us where to look, a watching audience is less likely to become lost in the film's action, even at its intense pace. A film just from Ross's viewpoint would have a different feel altogether: with Bourne, we stay just about in control. While we are sometimes watching Bourne react to Vosen's moves, often Bourne acts seemingly *ahead* of Vosen, as if anticipating him. The buzz is to see the world at Bourne's pace, or at least to try: in the act of processing so much information at speed, in fact, we can't help feeling a bit like Bourne ourselves.

Skimming and scanning

For Romney, the business of processing accelerated information is the real subject of the film. The human here has to compete with the speed and coverage of information technology massed against him. There is no time to plan moves: the search now is for 'the microscopic glitch, the nanosecond's delay that will allow Bourne to slip the net'.[30] We'll see other examples of this later in the film, though it is significant how much of an emphasis the film places on technology in general, and the ability in particular to comprehend bursts and pockets of information. Look, for example, at the way the next scene with Bourne is filmed. Using the notes he took from Ross (who is now dead, taken out by Paz), Bourne logs on in an internet café. We see an extreme close-up as he scans Ross's notepad for significant information, then follows this up by searching online for a particular named location (as it turns out, a safehouse used by Daniels, Ross's source). Note the way that the key address for the Madrid office, Bourne's subsequent destination, is shown: over Bourne's blurred shoulder, isolated by its white background to one side of the frame. Bourne's shoulder then moves across a bit more, thereby blacking out everything except the address, and in particular the word 'Madrid', which provides a visual clue to the next location (Fig 8 and 9). The following movement of Bourne across the whole screen serves to end the scene by effectively wiping it black. What the film does here is create a kind of accidental 'iris' and 'iris-in'; an iris being the use of a blackened border to isolate a circle within the image, a technique often used in silent cinema to highlight details or close scenes. It's an old technique then, but done subtly and at pace, and made to seem accidental. It's interesting, though, because it harks back to a form of storytelling without sound, in which the viewer has to scan the visual image to understand events.

Fig 8: Bourne's head in silhouette creates a makeshift 'iris', emphasising key information...

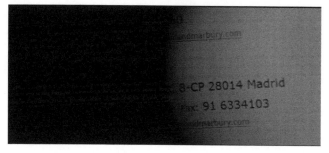

Fig 9: before creating an 'iris –in' with a movement towards the right.

This is appropriate for *Ultimatum*, where skimming and scanning the visible world is a key to survival. Another example of this approach can be seen in the film's first chase sequence, half way into the film, in which Bourne tries to intercept Desh in Tangiers. Bourne is fleeing the chasing police on a stolen motorbike, when his route is abruptly cut off. From a shot of Bourne coming to a stop, we cut to a handheld camera picking up Bourne's point of view. This camera makes a series of quick movements, stopping for a split second on the edge of a raised sidewalk and a loosened kerbstone (Fig 10 and 11). Again, this happens so quickly that we may not immediately work out the significance. But when we cut back to Bourne accelerating towards the kerbstone, using it to propel the bike up onto the raised edge and away from his pursuers, the images add up (Fig 12). Like much of the earlier Waterloo sequence, then, things only make sense *in retrospect*. This emphasises the idea of things happening at pace, and the importance of speedy perception and decision-making. But in the surprise it can generate, it also allows us to experience the pleasure of rapid information processing.

Fig 10: A point-of-view shot pans quickly to focus on a raised sidewalk...

Fig 11: then pans down to focus on a loose kerbstone.

Fig 12: The bike jump then 'adds up' the previous shots.

To return finally to the question of mimesis, and the kind of reality *Ultimatum* looks to represent, we can conclude that this 'skim and scan' style is the best way to evoke a reality where barely noticeable details and the rapid flow of information are key. As we saw in the last chapter, the *Bourne* series looks to evoke a world in which things of real consequence to our everyday world happen without our knowledge. The fact that *Ultimatum* revels in the full range of intelligence and surveillance machinery – identity databanks, keyword identification software, CCTV linked to high-speed networks – emphasises the role of covert technology in the policing of our daily existence. Mastery of our own lives, let alone the world, is from this perspective a complex business, one which requires a knowledge and mastery of this same technology. For the modern action hero, being tough is not enough. Today's sexiest action heroes need to be technically savvy as well as slick.

The point that *Ultimatum* wants to make, then, like many espionage thrillers, is that the world and its workings cannot so easily be understood. But to show the difficulty of perceiving the world requires that cinema should itself be challenging: this is because cinema itself is a form of seeing, and also a medium, literally a mid-point between the world and the viewer. This is why our skills of perception are taken to the limit in this film. But with Bourne to point us in the direction, the ride is a thrilling one.

Close-up: 'He's picking us apart'

In the middle of the Waterloo sequence, a grab team at the rear of a food store tries to take out Ross, only for Bourne to intervene and take them out. This short scene is a good example both of *Ultimatum*'s fast-cutting style and its approach to filming action. As we'll see, it disproves the idea that filming action is either easy or unintelligent. By contrast, we can see that filming a short fight sequence may involve a variety of directorial choices, together with a complex approach to editing, and a sharp awareness of how to maintain the viewer's attention.

We join the action at the point where Ross, as directed by Bourne, has gone through the back of the store (approximately 22 minutes and 52 seconds into the film): Bourne has watched as the members of the grab team descend on the rear of the store with the aim to intercept Ross.

We see Ross making toward the rear exit stairs, at which point one of the grab team (GT1) appears at the bottom of the screen. A close-up, point-of-view (POV) shot from Ross's perspective sees GT1 aiming his weapon. A cut back to the original set-up sees Bourne appear from the same point at GT1 and disarm him: following this, a closer shot shows Bourne disable GT1, while in a reverse angle Ross flinches. In the POV shot again, Bourne turns to face Ross.

A new camera angle and new line of action is initiated as Bourne runs up the stairs, passing Ross and pushing him aside: as yet, the object of Bourne's attention is not clear to us, which therefore maintains tension and expectation within the scene. As the camera pans right with Bourne's movement, we see the second member of the grab team (GT2) appear through an upper doorway. As Ross crashes into the wall at the base of the stairs, we return to Bourne striking GT2 (Fig 13), the impact of which is shown in another shot, 90 degrees left of the previous one. Surprise is then added to the sequence, as the camera pans rapidly to the right, revealing a third member of the team (GT3) appearing through the opposite doorway, his gun already drawn. This use of space to spring momentary surprises, along with the temporary concealment of Bourne's objectives and targets, will be a key feature of later action sequences. We cut back to a medium shot as Bourne traps GT3's gun arm, and then, from a closer angle, twists him round and swings him (Fig 14).

Fig 13: Bourne strikes one member of the grab team...

Fig 14: then deals with another on a different line of action.

In the return medium shot we see GT3 crash into GT2, incapacitating the former. A series of brief shots then shows GT2 recovering to wrestle Bourne, sending him into a wall. Bourne is able to use his right elbow to strike GT2. The scene then builds on its elements of tension and surprise as, in a tight shot over Bourne's shoulder, a fourth team member (GT4) appears (Fig 15). A reverse angle shows GT4 approaching Bourne from behind, gun drawn, at which point Bourne turns, placing GT2 between him and GT4. Another medium close-up over Bourne's shoulder shows us the gun being aimed by GT4, at which point the reverse angle reveals the body of GT2 being used to keep the gun away from Bourne (Fig 16). We then return to the previous angle, where we see Bourne's hand disarm GT4, sending the gun to the floor.

Fig 15: A new line of action reveals the threat of a new attacker...

Fig 16: ...who Bourne disarms.

As a reminder both of the situation, but also of further trajectories of potential attack, we draw back now to Ross, shot from over the shoulder, looking on as Bourne fights. He looks over his shoulder in the direction of the viewer. A medium shot returns to Bourne, who incapacitates GT4. He then returns to GT2, who is still standing. We see Bourne turn to GT2 in close-up, before a cut to a low-angle medium shot sees Bourne throw him over onto the stairwell. There is then a slight pause to gather breath, as we watch Bourne retrieve the various weapons. A close rapid pan then follows Bourne using the gun to knock out GT2, signaling the end of the fight.

A shot–reverse-shot exchange shows Bourne looking at Ross, who stares back. As is typical in the film, moments of violence are ended with silence. Finally, Bourne looks up: as a POV shot, the camera zooms in to focus on a CCTV camera (Fig 17). We then return to the New York hub, where the image from the camera is relayed back to Vosen and his deputy, Wills. Bourne 'looks' for the first time at his remote adversary who now, in turn, looks back at him.

Figure 17 The surveillance camera view signals the end of the fight, and reveals Bourne to Vosen.

Vosen: My God. That's Jason Bourne.

Wills: He's picking us apart.

(Length of sequence: 35 seconds. Number of shots: 35. ASL: one second.)

As we see, a sequence filmed within the bounds of rapid editing can be detailed and thoughtfully constructed, especially in the way it plays with onscreen and offscreen space, together with point of view, to create tension and surprise. Its evocation of Bourne's anticipation and spatial awareness at speed is a signature of the film and its main protagonist. We also see how this scene is not just a gratuitous spectacle of action, but serves as a key moment in the narrative, as it brings Bourne and Vosen 'face to face', resulting in Vosen's order to execute Bourne along with Ross (we will look further at the relationship between action and narration in Chapter Six).

Footnotes

17. Stendhal, *The Charterhouse of Parma*, trans. Margaret Mauldon (Oxford: Oxford University Press, 1997), p. 49.

18. Matthew Potolsky, *Mimesis* (London and New York: Routledge, 2006), p. 1.

19. Maltby, *Hollywood Cinema*, pp. 231–232.

20. Stendhal, *Scarlet and Black*, trans. Margaret Shaw (Harmondsworth: Penguin, 1953), p. 365.

21. Bordwell, *Narration in the Fiction Film*, pp. 4–10.

22. Greengrass's use of a red bus and the London Underground in *Ultimatum* is possibly a response to the idealised representation of London we find in films such as *Bridget Jones' Diary* (2001) and *Love, Actually* (2003) (the idea of 'red bus' as a descriptive category for exportable British films is highlighted in John Fitzgerald, *Studying British Cinema: 1999–2009* [Leighton Buzzard: Auteur, 2010], pp. 47–72]). A red double-decker bus was blown up in the co-ordinated terrorist bombings of July 2005; the same month that an unarmed Brazilian man, Jean Charles de Menezes, in a case of mistaken identity, was shot dead by police on a London underground train.

23. John Silberg, 'Bourne Again', *American Cinematographer*, 88.9 (September 2007).

24. Bordwell, *The Way Hollywood Tells It*, p. 121.

25. Bordwell, *ibid.*

26. Bordwell, *ibid.*, p. 260.

27. Bordwell, *ibid.*, p. 123.

28. Jonathan Romney, review of The Bourne Ultimatum, *The Independent on Sunday*, 19 August 2007.

29. Romney, *ibid.*

30. Romney, *ibid.*

Summary and questions

- Cinema is essentially a 'mimetic' art and is therefore interested in trying to 'imitate' or represent reality in some way.

- Representing contemporary reality requires us to incorporate things such as surveillance culture, the awareness of being watched as well as watching.

- *The Bourne Ultimatum* uses the Waterloo sequence as a showcase for its stylistic choices. It uses mobile cameras and fast-cutting approaches to editing in order to capture the speed and urgency of Bourne's situation.

- As a result, the film synthesises the style of contemporary action cinema with broader social/political themes, without either aspect being compromised.

- Consider different approaches to camerawork and editing style. What might be gained or lost in filming *Ultimatum* with more still cameras and slower editing?

- Do you agree with critics who suggest that the film manages to be thrilling and intellectually exciting at the same time? How does it do this? Can you think of other films that achieve the same results?

- How can we explain the film's constant emphasis on vision and information? Do you see this as representative of our contemporary world at all?

Chapter Four: From Superman to Invisible Man – Bourne and the City

As we saw earlier, part of the appeal of Bourne as a character is that he always seems one step ahead. This is partially a trick of cinema: limit what we can see as viewers, but allow the protagonist a less limited knowledge of his environment. The result is that the viewer of the film is always kept alert, watching for outcomes and different turns of events, but rarely able to anticipate them. What makes this especially exciting in the case of the *Bourne* films is that Jason Bourne seems to discover his skills almost as he goes along: when it happens, it just happens, as if his body remembers it before his mind does.

Take the example of the rooftop chase sequence in Tangiers, which takes place just past the middle point of the film. Bourne, if we remember, is trying to track down the Blackbriar operative Desh. Desh has just killed Neal Daniels – Ross's source, and the man Bourne was trying to reach – and has now been sent by Vosen to track down Bourne's friend, and CIA employee, Nicky Parsons. Desh, possibly thinking that Bourne was killed in the explosion that killed Daniels, follows Nicky into the dense and twisty streets of the old city. Not only has Desh got the jump on Bourne, but Bourne, who has just ridden a stolen motorbike through the pedestrian quarter, is trying to shake off the local police force, who believe that he is the bomber. Knowing that Desh will kill Nicky if he fails to intercept him, Bourne is forced to take the direct route, bypassing the labyrinth of ground level in favour of the rooftops themselves. He starts to run, hurdling and vaulting obstacles where necessary, the policemen in pursuit. Sprinting through washing lines, he grabs several handfuls of clothes and towels. This action is not immediately explained to us, whereas in a lot of narrative cinema it would be. At last all becomes clear when, his hands now wrapped in the stolen washing, he pulls himself over a high wall whose top is defensively lined with a layer of broken glass. His pursuers, lacking Bourne's ability to foresee what is ahead, are left behind.

The fun here is to see the inexplicable suddenly explained, and to see the payoff for the protagonist. It evokes Bourne's apparent mastery of his environment: his almost extra-sensory powers of prediction and GPS-like attunement to the variations of space. If we wanted to be cynical, of course, we might say that there's no way he could anticipate such a thing, just as no one can mentally second-guess the combined mass of Waterloo's CCTV cameras. Fair enough; but then, a totally believable Bourne wouldn't be half as much fun. More importantly, though, Bourne's vision is unbelievable because *no one can see like this*, which is one of the main points of the film. As with the Waterloo sequence, the idea is that the world is at some level beyond our ability to see, and therefore beyond our ability to fully understand and master (while many films, by contrast, trade in the comforting idea of seeing and knowing everything). Bourne is designed to show up the deficiencies in our own vision when compared with the complexity and threat of the world.

The superhero and realism

Does this make Jason Bourne a kind of superhero? In a way it does. Superman's X-ray vision means that walls and obstacles are no barrier to sight, even if (in the earlier *Superman* films at least) he uses it mostly for looking at Lois Lane's underwear. Superman, like his friend and occasional adversary Batman, also likes to use elevated vantage points to keep an eye on the city below, scanning it for those unexplained changes in movement that mean crime is taking place. And special abilities? Bourne certainly shares some of Spider-Man's agility and Daredevil's uncanny sense of space (*Daredevil*, 2003); while his mastery of technology, even if it is more low-tech, would appeal to Tony Stark, otherwise known as Iron Man.

There's an important difference, though. If modern superhero movies such as *The Dark Knight* (2008) or *Iron Man* (2008) make reference to real-world events, touching on questions of politics and ethics, this is done within the superhero genre, along with its more fantastical conventions and particular relationship to truth. Narratives about people with superpowers are the most popular form of contemporary myth, not just dominating our multiplex screens, but also featuring prominently on mainstream television (*Smallville* (WB/CW, 2001–2011), *Heroes* (NBC, 2006–2010), *True Blood* [HBO, 2008–]), best-selling fiction (the *Harry Potter* and *Twilight* books), as well being the basis for countless videogames. Unless the Ministry of Magic has managed to pull the wool over my Muggle eyes, these kinds of people do not (yet!) exist; but this is not so much beside the point – it *is* the point. The appeal of these characters is their ability to do more than is actually possible in the real world, and as such, they make manifest the desire on our part to be able to do these things. There is in this sense a 'utopian' aspect to these narratives, in the way they give imaginary presence to a world that is ideal and unrealisable; and this is why they are never just 'escapist', to use the much-overused term.[31]

It's no accident that, in the light of anxieties produced by events such as the 9/11 or 7/7 attacks, 'the city in danger' has become a key fictional motif, seeping into genres traditionally associated with unreal or non-terrestrial worlds (especially as a large proportion of viewers and readers live in big cities like the ones the stories describe). For secret-agent shows such as 24 or the BBC's *Spooks* (2002–2011), we expect to see men and women in black working their way through an urban jungle; but the city is as much under threat in the later *Harry Potter* films, which have a very recognisable London for much of their setting, just as it is in the first series of *Heroes*, which has New York as its narrative centre.[32]

For vintage heroes like Batman and Superman, in fact, the city is not just where they live; it shapes and defines them, especially as their self-determined remit is to protect 'their' respective cities. The creators of these characters made this connection clear when they created fictional cities for them: Batman's Gotham, Superman's Metropolis. In a fascinating book on superheroes in the comics and films of the last century, Scott Bukatman points out that the aerial, panoramic view aspired to by early superheroes – Batman's rooftop perch, Superman's urban hovering – was always one of control, watching over an urban sprawl that was beyond visible mastery; a perspective which, in the process, emphasised the superhero's intimate and obsessive relationship to the city.[33] In the Batman movies too, we notice how much emphasis is placed on the architecture of Gotham: a space which dominates the action almost as much as the characters themselves,[34] whether it's the shadowy, gothic excesses of Tim Burton's 1989 version, or the IMAX-shot granite, glass and steel of Christopher Nolan's 2008 re-vision (much of which is filmed on location in Chicago). As we'll see below, *Ultimatum* makes use of the space, and especially the heights, of the city, though not in a way which draws attention to the city in itself, as *The Dark Knight* does. The type of establishing shots of the city that are a staple of this type of cinema – like the slow tracking shot onto the cityscape that opens Nolan's film – are generally omitted in *Ultimatum*, which situates its protagonist quickly within the action.

Bourne is not in a position to contemplate the sights of the city, but this is not his thing anyway. Bukatman's point about the aerial super-view is that it is also linked to a form of policing. This is exactly what Christian Bale's Batman does at the end of *The Dark Knight*, with his machine that visualises the whole city, bat-like, by converting sound waves into images (a machine that causes the ethically-minded Lucius Fox, played by Morgan Freeman, to tender his resignation). This kind of software is a counter-terrorist unit's fantasy, but therefore the sort of gadgetry Jason Bourne would have to evade at all costs. Does this indicate a key difference between Greengrass's film and those like Nolan's?

The Dark Knight is, in truth, ambivalent toward its protagonist's actions, stressing throughout that it is the public men of law like Commissioner Gordon and Harvey Dent who are better placed to be the city's heroes. But it is also very much about the experience of the post-9/11 city. Immediate post-9/11 superhero films, such as *Spider-Man 2* (2004) and Pixar's *The Incredibles* (2004), focused their narrative around the threat to the American city (New York itself in *Spider-Man 2*), partly representing how the city comes together to repel terror; just as *The Dark Knight*, whose imagery much more explicitly evokes terror attacks or a state of war (a panicking public leaving the city, the constant proximity of fire trucks and police), climaxes with the citizens, and even its convicts, forming a more-or-less unified response to the danger. In *Ultimatum*, meanwhile, the city is mostly an anonymous venue for Bourne's work, for the simple reason that saving New York (and, by implication, America) is not the main point of the film. As we saw previously, the *Bourne* series, and *Ultimatum* above all, takes pains to depict the long reach of near-invisible intelligence forces around the globe, be it Munich, Moscow or Madrid – and also Manhattan (emphasised by the geometric patterns and tracing lines that are a feature of the series' end credits). Unsurprisingly, then, given Greengrass's approach in *United 93*, there is a judicious balance in the film, in that New York is just one of many cities in the world, rather than *the* city.

Horizontality

This is also a world that is contained by gravity. Everyone knows Superman can fly, but what really distinguishes the modern superhero film even from its earlier incarnations – thanks largely to innovations in special effects technology – is the way things operate *vertically*.[35] Whether it's Superman or Iron Man, or Neo in the *Matrix* films (1999–2003), these are characters that make use of their ability to defy earthly limitations, rocketing skywards either in play or in battle. We might thrill to the verticality of modern super-cinema, with its rocketing and plunging down-to-earth thrills, but this is not possible in the world of Bourne, where more earth-bound flights are needed. When Bourne enters the old city to intercept Desh and save Nicky, his only option is to think *horizontally*: to find the most direct route across and through the labyrinth that confronts him at the beginning of the pursuit (Fig 18).

Fig 18: Bourne surveys the rooftops that must be crossed to save Nicky.

The mission: to get across the city from point A to point B, using not the route marked on the map, but the most direct one available to the agile human body. Before Jason Bourne came up with this plan, it was already being practised in the real world in the now well-known form of parkour. The term for this type of urban sport, which involves negotiating various urban obstacles and barriers via the use of leaps, vaults and climbs, comes originally from the French noun *parcours*: a word which refers both to a kind of assault course, but also to the trajectory traced by an individual in their movement through space. Beyond its status as an urban and online phenomenon, first in France and then all over the world, parkour and its relative 'free-running' have provided inspiration for many recent films, and action sequences in particular: most prominently in the District 13 films (Banlieue 13 in the original French) – *District 13* (2004) and *District 13– Ultimatum* (2009) – and in the early chase sequence in *Casino Royale*.

Parkour politics

As a technique and visual style for the earth-bound superhero, parkour is a perfect solution. Practitioners of parkour or free-running see themselves as stretching the laws and limitations of gravity through their various moves, but also defying the constraints of the world around them. Walls to a free-runner or parkour *traceur* are an opportunity for creation, rather than a barrier to movement. The city's buildings and passageways, its various confined urban spaces, become sites whose meaning and purpose are therefore reinvented.[36] It's no surprise that for some practitioners, such as *Casino Royale*'s Sébastian Foucan, much of their inspiration comes from those movies whose gravity-defying moves they want to emulate in the real world: films like *The Matrix*, which is based on a premise that our actions are limited mostly by our lack of imagination.

There's a paradox here of course: the stunts performed by Foucan in the Bond film, or by parkour specialist David Belle in the *District 13* movies, appeal to us because they emulate for real what the makers of *The Matrix* simulate with wires and CGI. They excite our imaginations because they're actually doing it, and because their jumps and vaults are *not* created through the type of computer-imaging which, increasingly, can cause us to question whether or not what we see is real. How all this feeds into *Ultimatum*, then, is to give the film an increased quality of realism, which as we've seen throughout this book is vital to its themes. It works to further associate the hero with physical and mental resources, against the hardware and software that are available to his adversaries.

While parkour lends itself obviously to chases across rooftops, and extraordinary feats of human agility, there is a philosophical and even political side to it as well. Parkour sees obstacles as possibilities, and therefore refuses to accept that people should be both contained and defined by their surroundings. Parkour does not seek to break any laws; it doesn't threaten property or buildings, but merely refuses to accept that the places in which we live and move have only one use or meaning. This gives it a political dimension even at its most playful, given the backdrop of surveillance and policing in which many of us live, and which is of course at the heart of *Ultimatum*. To go back to the Waterloo sequence, when we look at it closely, we see how often Matt Damon is filmed moving across the camera at different angles, rather than head on. Sometimes he even appears to flash past the camera in the opposite direction to the camera's movement, as if evading the camera altogether. This emphasises the chess game, made up of angles and trajectories of defence and attack, that Bourne is playing with the CCTV system. And this, too, is a kind of parkour, even within the confines of London's busiest train station.

The idea that simply getting around the city is a kind of tactical game is a central one in the Bourne series, and especially in *Ultimatum*. New York, and more specifically Manhattan, represents the ideal challenge to Bourne's skills: a vast urban space, both horizontally and vertically, but one that is rigidly organised into an easily readable pattern of streets and avenues. On his return to New York, Bourne is not just out for a stroll: he is after Landy's help, and Vosen's carefully guarded secrets. His means of achieving this depends on his sense of the city spaces and his movement through them.

Hide and seek

Bourne's skills echo here those of his adversary, Paz, who we saw in the earlier London sequence. Once again, the rapid processing of urban information in order to create an advantage is key: in this case, the scanning of occupied levels in a high-rise building, and the disappearance into these unknown spaces of the city, the pockets of refuge from the crowds and the eyes of surveillance (Fig 19). If Bourne was Superman in Morocco, in Manhattan he wants to be the invisible man. There is, of course, a plausibility issue here, which the more sceptical viewers of the film might point out. Bourne turns up in New York under a barely-traceable fake name, one we might recognise from the cluster of fake passports he finds in *The Bourne Identity*; yet he walks through security and onwards to a taxi like no one could care less. Seeing as he's a wanted man, with the forces of CIA intelligence on his case, shouldn't he make more effort to hide his appearance? Why, in short, doesn't Bourne go undercover?

Fig 19:
Hiding
in the
shadows
of the city.

This is a good question. Before heading to New York, we see Bourne seeing off Nicky, now a fugitive, at a coach station in Morocco. We've also just seen her cutting and dyeing her hair, in a way which echoes Marie's own change of appearance in the first film (this is a very deliberate echo: it's hinted at in *Ultimatum* that Bourne and Nicky used to have a relationship, though, of course, Bourne can't remember it). Physical transformation typically goes hand in hand with being on the run, and the *Bourne* films observe the rule where the female characters are concerned. The odd thing is that Bourne himself ignores these rules, sticking to his black combo and close-cropped, clean-shaven look throughout. Wouldn't it make more sense for a rogue operative on a CIA death list to mix things up a bit? Grow a moustache, get some dreadlocks, or at least try out some different colours? Doesn't Jason Bourne, in fact, stick out like a sore thumb?

In a way, yes. Credibility goes a bit out of the window where Bourne's appearance is concerned. Does it matter? I'd say it doesn't. In Robert Ludlum's original novels, there is the suggestion that Bourne's appearance has constantly changed, either through disguise or reconstructive surgery. This would be a logical practice for covert political assassins. But real-world or literary logic is not always logical for the purposes of cinema. The problem with the Master of Disguise as a movie character, at least one we are supposed to follow, is that we will always recognise the actor behind the disguise. This makes them look, if we follow this logic, like a very *bad* Master of Disguise, and in turn makes the other unsuspecting characters seem a bit witless. One alternative is to hide the actor completely, like the sequence in *The Silence of the Lambs* (1991) – spoiler alert! – where Hannibal Lecter escapes from jail wearing a dead policeman's face. This works brilliantly in that particular film, though it's used for surprise and shock value. Which is why, when we need to follow the character in disguise, contemporary films tend to have a jokey, cartoony feel (like Spielberg's *Catch Me if You Can* [2002]), or are intentionally daft (as in the Pink Panther movies [1963–2009], and their absurd Inspector Clouseau).

Keeping Bourne in his (anti-)costume is therefore a way of maintaining a consistent look for the character, but also an acknowledgement that we take our heroes more seriously when we see them just as they are. It's not just that Matt Damon would look silly running around in a wig (though he clearly would). It's more a case of one kind of non-realism being traded in for another. That isn't the whole story, though. The point about the world of the *Bourne* films is that other people, and most significantly such forces as the CIA, are generally not witless, but resourceful men and women with intelligent tools at their disposal. The series doesn't bother disguising Bourne because – forgetting Nicky's black bob for the moment – it wouldn't make any difference. This at least is what the films want us to believe. It also puts a greater emphasis on the skill of the protagonist to evade detection and capture, without the use of corny devices like false beards or funny accents. What's more, it demonstrates Bukatman's point that in the modern day wearing a mask – 'hiding' your identity, in other words – is the most obvious way of drawing attention to yourself.[37] In the big city, the most effective mask is just to look normal: dress down, blend in with the crowds, seek out the shadows.

Picking up on my earlier point about the city, we notice in the New York scenes how the camerawork emphasises the human body in the city, rather than the city itself. It does this through the use of long shots and long lenses, which allow us to pick out Landy as she walks through the busy city streets; or in the way the camera shoots her and Bourne in low-angle shots, showing how the verticality of New York looms over its inhabitants (Fig 20). Whereas many New York movies choose to highlight the city's well-known sights (such as the Empire State and Chrysler buildings), here there are mainly anonymous blocks, or fairly characterless transport hubs such as the Port Authority Terminal. We've already seen how Bourne makes use of these buildings as a vantage point and a place to disappear. It's from here that he makes the phone call – a repeat of the sequence that ended *Supremacy* – in which Landy gives Bourne his real name, as well as a coded address for the Treadstone training facility where the film will reach its climax.

Fig 20: Walking in New York, shot from low angles to emphasise the 'vertical' city.

The film will also make Bourne literally disappear and reappear: not in a puff of smoke, but in a game of cinematic space and misinformation. Vosen's team intercept a text message sent to Landy's phone: an instruction to meet at Tudor City, in Manhattan's East Side. Both Landy and Vosen's team converge on this location, with the film cross-cutting from Vosen in the car to Bourne entering another building. Films are usually edited in this way with a particular logic of time and space: cross-cutting like this often builds up anticipation, for when all the parties meet at the spot designated within the narrative. The trick here is that Bourne, it turns out, is somewhere else altogether: if we are fooled at this point, it's because the film exploits both the grammar of film-making, and the anonymity of modern city space, to make us assume Bourne is in the same part of town (a technique used stunningly to similar effect, in fact, near the end of *The Silence of the Lambs*). Vosen realises his error when Bourne, who we see looking at microfilm, calls him on his cell phone. Vosen flounders and requests a meeting, telling Bourne that right now he is in his office. 'I doubt that', replies Bourne: 'If you were in your office we'd be having this conversation face-to-face.' Realisation turns to astonishment on Vosen's part, and maybe the viewer's, as the camera, in a shift from close-up to medium shot, confirms Bourne's presence in Vosen's own room. It's a great line from Bourne, and a great moment, one in which the film plays and sounds like an old-fashioned action movie. It's also perhaps a pointless and dangerous thing to say, especially for someone as cautious as Bourne, given that it now brings the weight of Vosen's forces crashing down on Bourne's head. But then, we expect nothing less from a Bourne film: forget plausibility for a moment, and let the chase begin!

Footnotes

31. Michael Chabon's Pulitzer Prize-winning novel *The Amazing Adventures of Kavalier and Clay* (2000), a terrific meditation on the values of escapism, is the story of two comic-book writers in New York, against the backdrop of the second world war. Their lock-busting superhero creation, symbolically, is called 'The Escapist'.

32. On the release of the seventh *Harry Potter* film in London in November 2010, it was impossible not to notice the use of the capital's buildings in the posters advertising the film. *Heroes*, meanwhile, though basically inspired by the *X-Men* comic and film series, looked to underline the 'ordinary' nature of its protagonists; most notably that of Peter Petrelli,the series' central character, whose status as a New York paramedic connected him to the 'ordinary heroes' that died in the 9/11 attacks.

33. Scott Bukatman, *Matters of Gravity: Special Effects and Supermen in the Twentieth Century* (Durham: Duke University Press, 2003), pp. 188–203.

34. I owe this observation to my editor, John Atkinson.

35. Kristen Whissel, 'Tales of Upward Mobility', *Film Quarterly*, 59.4 (2006), 23–34.

36. Neil Archer, 'Virtual Poaching and Altered Space: Reading Parkour in French Visual Culture', *Modern & Contemporary France*, 18.1 (2010), 93–107.

37. Bukatman, *op cit.*, pp. 213–214.

Summary and questions

- *The Bourne Ultimatum* is particularly interested in the idea of negotiating urban space.

- The film draws on elements of parkour at times to explore this idea.

- We might see Bourne as a kind of urban superhero, operating on a horizontal (as opposed to vertical) plane.

- *Ultimatum* rejects the possibility of disguise, thinking instead about how the hero evades detection and capture using their sense of the city's spaces.

- How does the use/non-use of CGI affect the way we watch a film? Do you think the absence of intensive CGI in *Ultimatum* added to its popularity?

- Why do you think the *Bourne* films in general are so interested in city spaces?

Chapter Five: Almost Too Close for Comfort – Punch-ups and Pile-ups

As we saw in the introduction, the action film for some is the lowest of film genres. But whether or not action movies attract either contempt or devotion, those in either camp tend to focus on the same thing: action as spectacle. For critics of action cinema, there is too much action. For fans, action is the source of the fun. Critics might respond that this preference for action is at the expense of cinema's classical narrative values: story, characterisation, social comment. Fans might then reply that they are not interested in such things. And so on. It's not that both parties are wrong exactly. It's just that neither view takes into account that action movies are never just 'action'.

My point in this chapter is not simply that the most action-packed action movie still has some kind of story. To say this would suggest that action is always to the side of the narrative, which would not help us understand what action really *does*. I want to suggest, then, that action does not stop narrative in its tracks, like a kind of musical interlude. In fact, and especially in the case of *Ultimatum*, it is a vital part of the narrative, something that initiates, develops, or often brings to a climax events in the story.[38] In this way, action sequences can have the impact of a key piece of dialogue, a moment of revelation, or a dramatic confrontation. All this *besides* simply looking great.

It's also worth pointing out that what we call 'action' is not always obvious. We can argue, in fact, that action in cinema is not defined by a particular thing that is shown, but by the *effect* of the thing shown. If we consider the Waterloo sequence discussed in Chapter Three, for example, we can see how little of it comprises 'action' in its most conventional sense: a few brief bursts of fighting, and a foot-chase at the end. Ross's killing, meanwhile, in a deliberate reversal of action-movie style, is actually shown from far off - and therefore, from a certain point of view, not really 'action', despite its dramatic effect. At the same time, the impact generated by Ross's death at the end of the extended Waterloo scene, because of its significance within the sequence's narrative, underlines what I want to argue here: namely, that the feeling of the action – and for it to qualify as action, it surely has to be *felt*, not just seen – comes mainly through the editing and the tension it helps evoke, building up to (and momentarily released by) the shooting itself.

The Waterloo sequence, in other words, is an example of narrative *as action*, its dynamic coming from the dramatic qualities it generates. The emotional effect of action is here connected, significantly, to threat. It's clear that in a film with the realist and political aims of *Ultimatum*, action should not be just exciting spectacle, but something related more urgently to the film's wider themes. For the action to have any impact, it must unsettle as much as it excites. Some time after the release of Ultimatum, a person I spoke to about the film complained that there was something uncomfortable about it: the fight scenes in particular, he said, were *too close*. This is revealing, given that he wasn't sitting near any real punches, but near a screen with projected images and recorded sound. One of the things we need to look at, then, is how this feeling of closeness is created. As I'll show, this kind of intimacy in *Ultimatum*'s action scenes is both a means of exploring the film's themes, but is also a vital part of its storytelling.

Keeping it 'real'

Let's take, for example, Bourne's fight with Desh in Tangiers. What makes this scene so striking is the relentlessness of both participants. This is fighting up close with no breaks, no sparring, and no posing; where anything that comes to hand – a razor and a standing ashtray, but also a book, a tile or a towel – serves as a weapon. But we need to think also about the stakes of the fight. It's not just Nicky's life that's in the balance here: it's Bourne's, and also Desh's. We know that Treadstone and Blackbriar ops fight to kill, not incapacitate; and what's more, they die hard. From the moment Bourne begins to grapple with Desh, we know that one of them cannot get up again. Anyone who's ever watched professional boxing knows how hard it is to physically knock a trained fighter out cold, and in any case this would hardly be much use: Desh would come back for Bourne and Nicky, just as Paz comes back for Bourne towards the end of the film.

The intensity of this duel to the death is underscored by the speed at which both participants operate. The principles of rapid processing and response we looked at in Chapter Three are carried over into the more up-front action scenes such as this one. Note the way that Bourne in particular has to improvise rapidly with objects that come to hand: the way a hardback book is used, first with the spine to momentarily choke Desh, then flipped over to spread the impact of Bourne's punch, all in the space of a second. Or how, when the fight shifts its axis into the bathroom, the camera hovers momentarily overhead as Bourne hurls random bits of the shower unit at his oncoming assailant: nothing that in itself will do any real damage, but enough of a distraction to buy Bourne vital moments in the battle.

We also notice in the fight how much impact the various blows appear to have. Punches often land with dense thuds; the ashtray wielded like a club by Desh rings out metallically; towels and razor blades whip and whistle through the air. This is just a trick, of course; a cinematic illusion of violence, like all screen fights are. In reality, the two actors here are performing a series of closely choreographed moves, using rubberised props in place of real objects. The real work of the scene is done in the close-up camerawork, the editing, but above all in the use of sound. The clattering bursts that punctuate the fight scene are not sourced from the action, because there isn't any. They are what the business calls 'foley' sound: noises recorded and refined for a specific purpose, then layered onto the film soundtrack in post-production. It is this, combined with the movement of the camera that follows the various blows, that creates the feeling of closeness and impact. In the absence of real blows, and given that the film is only a two-dimensional image on a screen, amplified sound (relayed through the standard Dolby sound systems in modern cinemas) creates a strong imaginary impression of physical contact, where the visual image can only show play-acting.

The film underlines the importance of action noise by cutting out all other sound from the audio track. Like most of the film, which typically for Hollywood movies uses a music track throughout, the rooftop pursuit preceding the fight is accompanied by John Powell's score. The music recedes slightly as Bourne finally closes in on Desh, until the moment at which Bourne leaps from one balcony to the next and crashes through the window. Other films at this point might ramp up the music for the fight, the climax of the sequence. *Ultimatum* does the exact opposite, letting the fight play without music, the sounds of the blows working instead as a kind of percussion. This gives the noises more space to make themselves felt, but there also seems to be another, more realist intention here. Rather than revelling in the defeat of the opponent, emphasising the moment of victory as a dramatic music score might do, the film has Desh's death played out against an absence of *anything*, save for his final squeezed breaths. This moment, in distinction from the rest of the fight, is held in shot for slightly longer; following which we see an exchange of wordless looks between Bourne and Nicky. Nicky's look at Desh's body echoes the same ghastly expression that we saw with Marie in *The Bourne Identity*, when she first sees someone die: one of nausea, not exhilaration. This is indicative of the film's more complex aims. From the point of view of the film's narrative, the death of Desh enables Bourne and Nicky to both survive and continue. This clearly satisfies the demands of the story, and presumably the desires of the viewer; but the film also dwells on the human cost of this breakthrough.

Up close and (first-)personal

Besides wishing to show the physical repercussions of violence – Desh's strangulated corpse, or the battered face of Paz after a vehicle pile-up – *Ultimatum* also takes pains (excuse the pun) to put the viewer up close to the action. One of the fundamental aspects of cinema, as we know, is that it is a third-person medium: we watch characters perform actions. This marks it as different, say, from the 'first-person' effect of many videogames, which play on the effect of looking and reacting from the viewpoint of a character, one that in practice is an avatar of the player themselves. It's one of the paradoxes of cinema that such first-person perspectives, vital to the experience of videogame play, sometimes have an opposite effect when used in narrative films. Any number of driving games offer windscreen points-of-view to simulate the driving experience, while titles such as *Grand Theft Auto* allow you to speed and crash any number of cars around a virtual New York, in the form of Liberty City. When you break it down to its component parts, the car chase in Bourne has all the ingredients of a *GTA* sequence: steal a cop car, race through downtown, avoid getting yourself shot to bits or having your engine explode.

In the case of *Ultimatum*, the character mission is straightforward: outrun and outwit Vosen's men, avoid and incapacitate Paz, and meet

Landy on East 71st Street. The limited perspective in a game chase adds to its exhilarating effect, as the focus is solely on the avatar's frontward and peripheral vision. But the focus of the game is accomplishing the task, which can take as long as is required: gameplay is not narrative in the cinematic sense, as the latter, to generate its effect, depends upon a specific duration in which its action takes place. If the game's camera changed angles or point of view in mid-chase, moreover, it would be distracting, interrupting the flow of the game. In cinema, by contrast, we are watching rather than being a character: we need to see them, not see through them. We also expect and demand the changes in camera views, not only to create more variety in the action, but to better convey the sense of space in which the action takes place.

Ultimatum's action scenes are very much in this cinematic tradition, rejecting the heavy use of CGI favoured by many contemporary blockbusters. The influence again is the realist aesthetic of 1970s Hollywood, and more specifically here the seminal New York car chase in William Friedkin's police movie *The French Connection* (1971). This film helped set a trend for future action movies in its rejection of processed shots, otherwise known as 'back projection': in other words, where the movement of the car is artificially simulated by projected shots of movement, usually behind studio-shot footage of the driver. *The French Connection* not only showed us actual driving, it also sought to bring its audience closer to the action, combining shots from outside the car with close-up shots of the driver in pursuit, POV shots from the driver's seat, and what we might call 'bumper-vision': a camera strapped to the very end of the car.[39] Dan Bradley, *Ultimatum*'s second-unit director (the person often in charge of shooting 'exterior' or 'landscape' shots in a film, but in this case also the stunt sequences), looked for innovative ways of combining spectacle and immersion in the same way as Friedkin's film. He did this by exploiting the filming technology involved – much of which can be seen in the DVD bonus material – along with the editing of the film in post-production.

As an example of this approach, let's return briefly to the Tangiers rooftop chase. We might recall the two occasions in which Bourne leaps from one window to another across narrow streets: the first sees him tumbling into a shocked family's home; the second is the climactic moment when he intercepts Desh. These leaps take up only a few seconds of screen time, but if we look at them carefully we see that they are made up of several shots from different angles. For the second jump, we first see Matt Damon running toward a balcony rail. This then cuts to a shot of his foot on the rail as he commences the leap, followed by a dramatic low-angle shot of Bourne leaping across the space (Fig 21). This cuts immediately to a shot of Bourne hurtling forwards and downwards toward the window, into which he then crashes (Fig 22), before a new set up shows the impact of the crash from inside the house. The dynamic shot that follows Bourne mid-leap was done by putting a second stuntman on a wire and harness, a lightweight camera held to his stomach, and having him leap behind the stuntman doubling for Bourne. In this way, the stunt team was able to capture the feel and movement of Bourne's leap, and subsequently insert it into the edited sequence. The result is that the stunt combines spectacle with immersion: the leap seen from a detached viewpoint, and then from the perspective of the character.

Fig 21: Bourne leaps, shot from below...

Fig 22: ... and then from behind, as we leap with him.

Throughout the New York car chase, similar techniques are used to position us as both observers of the action and participants in it. One of the recent innovations exploited by the *Bourne* series is the remote piloting of the motor vehicles. This takes the form of a pod attached to the front, back, or sometimes roof of the stunt car, from which the car is driven and steered: this allows the actor seated in the on-screen driver's seat to be filmed against an authentic moving background. While old-fashioned back projection is now unheard of, a more common option these days, both in television and film, is to shoot against a blue screen and to have the background inserted digitally (the typical practice in *24*, for example, where time and production demands do not allow for the complications of extensive location shooting). The more nuts-and-bolts approach in *Ultimatum* gives us a dirtier sense of realism, as well as allowing for complicated sequences such as the high-speed dueling between Bourne and Paz. It also puts us closer to Bourne when, in moments of collision, we shift instantaneously from the impact to Bourne's reaction, thrown forward together with the juddering camera.

At other points, the sequence takes a more in-your-face approach to immersive editing. At one point near the end of the chase, Paz forces a collision with another vehicle and Bourne's. We see the initial impact from an overhead shot (Fig 23), followed by a shot in which the front left of this other car races toward, and appears to smash into, the camera (Fig 24). Then a third set up – like much of the film, the stunts are filmed simultaneously from several cameras – shows the impact of this car on Paz's, with the fountain of shattered glass produced by it. This obviously happens too quickly to register in detail: shots such as that of the car apparently crashing into the camera are fractions of a second in duration. Yet they are still felt even if they can't be mentally processed; or even *because* they go unprocessed. In keeping with the general style of the film, these almost indecipherable bursts of action add to the film's sense of breathless pace, impacting almost literally on a viewer who is jolted and shaken alongside the film's protagonist.

Fig 23: A high-angle shot shows the impact of a three-way crash...

Fig 24: ... which sends one car heading at speed toward the camera.

In the sense that this chase is another kind of duel between operatives, it has to finish decisively – even if, in this instance, Bourne is able to leave Paz alive, and merely his car beyond resuscitation. This chase leaves its biggest stunt till last: a pinball-like collision in which Bourne's police car, rammed sideways-on up the road partition beneath an elevated train bridge, clips an oncoming van, sending it spinning round back onto Paz. It's an almost identical ending to the chase in *Supremacy*, which emphasises that the *Bourne* movies follow some basic generic templates, though the difference here is that Bourne uses his ingenuity to avoid the fate of Kirill in the previous film. Both vehicles here shoot headlong into the slowed traffic ahead, yet Bourne, in a trademark moment of lightning assessment and reflex, ducks and wraps himself in the passenger seat safety-belt. Of course, just how Bourne gets himself out of the fix is not the main interest here. We know he will, because he must; but the film rarely dwells on such matters. Instead, we get to admire the stunt itself in all its head-bashing, metal-crunching glory.

Just to reinforce the fact, we get to see it more than once. This is a cinematic trick undetectable to the eye in the immediate experience of the film. If we break down the shots in the film, we see Bourne's car pushed onto the road partition, into the path of the oncoming van. From this same perspective, we see Bourne's car hit from the rear, sending it spinning round onto Paz (Fig 25). We then see the two cars from an overhead reverse angle, with Bourne's vehicle continuing its movement, which will send Paz into the eventual pile-up (Fig 26). We then return not just to the previous set-up, but to the previous shot itself (Fig 27), flipping a second or so back in time. As any film student will know, this breaks the rules of cinematic continuity. Creating continuity in *Ultimatum*, though a difficult task because of its huge number of shots, is made easier due to its use of multiple cameras, which shoot the action simultaneously from different positions, along with the precise timing available in digital editing. So this mini-glitch in continuity, though barely noticeable, is clearly designed to create a specific effect. This 'temporal overlapping' of shots is in fact a staple of action movies, and especially in Hong Kong cinema, which has come to influence the way Hollywood action is shot.[40] In *Ultimatum*, this very discrete use of layering reinforces the stunt by making it fractionally longer. Like everything else in the film, it's all done in the blink of an eye. Yet it's enough to reiterate the impact of the stunt: a trick that emphasises for the viewer the force of the action, which might otherwise be over a bit too quickly.

Fig 25: Bourne's car, forced by Paz onto the partition, is clipped by an oncoming vehicle...

Fig 26: ... which turns Bourne's car over Paz's, seen from a reverse angle...

Fig 27: ... then we see the stunt again from the first angle.

Action as story

At this point, Bourne limps away to find Landy. It would be wrong to think, though, that at this point the film 'returned' to a story it had momentarily left behind. As I suggested at the beginning of this chapter, we should think instead of the action not as mere spectacle, but as a passage or process of the story itself. As Tico Romao has shown in his study of the car chase in Hollywood films, the chase can act as a key site both for plot development and dramatic interest; especially as the life-or-death aspect of the high-speed chase, and our interest in the protagonist's safe passage, creates suspense – a vital aspect of narrative.[41] In *Ultimatum*, we can see how the car chase and its resolution draw together key elements of the film's story: it brings into focus the various forces closing in on Bourne as he tries to reach his destination – a destination which is actually revealed, through cross-cutting between the roads and the CIA hub, during the chase sequence itself. It also brings Paz back into play, which ups the ante as far as Bourne's survival is concerned. It's also notable that the key plot information (the meaning of Landy's code, the location of Treadstone, and its relevance to the narrative as a whole) is revealed during the chase, meaning that Bourne's evasion of Paz and the other pursuers becomes vital from a narrative perspective.

As a final thought, we should also remind ourselves that the Bourne narrative is on one level an old-fashioned quest saga, a journey of one man to reach home and learn the truth. This situates the series within a tradition going as far back as ancient myths, and epic poems like Homer's *Odyssey*. If the latter is associated with 'classic' literature – in contrast to the *Bourne* series' connotation as 'airport fiction' or 'blockbuster' cinema – it's worth remembering how often in Homer's poem it is through action that the hero both progresses onto the next stage of the journey, and proves his worth as a protagonist. Presumably these descriptions of dynamic and spectacular action were and remain part of the long-term appeal of Homer's work, just as they are central to the popularity of the *Bourne* films. Yet in neither case is the narrative or dramatic value diminished by the introduction of action. Just the opposite, in fact.

Footnotes

38. Bordwell, *Hollywood*, pp. 104–105; also Geoff King, *Spectacular Narratives: Hollywood in the Age of the Blockbuster* (London and New York: I.B. Tauris, 2000), pp. 112–116.

39. For more on this film, and on the history of the Hollywood car chase more generally, see Tico Romao, 'Guns and Gas: Investigating the 1970s Car Chase Film', in Yvonne Tasker (ed), *Action and Adventure Cinema* (London and New York: Routledge, 2004), pp. 131–52.

40. See King, *op cit.*, pp. 93–97.

41. Romao, *op cit.*, p. 143.

Summary and questions

- *The Bourne Ultimatum* combines editing techniques with sound and point of view to create action that is at once immersive and intelligible from a narrative perspective.

- The film sometimes 'cheats' realism – for example, through the use of Foley sound or overlapping editing – to suggest greater impact.

- The action sequences in the film can be seen as integrated parts of the narrative, not 'interludes' within it.

- When you watch action films, do you watch 'only the action'? Is it possible to separate 'action' from 'story'?

- Consider the different options available for shooting action sequences in films: how do changes in editing speed or point of view affect the way the sequences are perceived? Are the choices in *Ultimatum* suitable ones?

- How might 'non-realistic' techniques of filming action scenes – additional sound effects, overlapping editing, even CGI – help to make them 'more realistic'?

Chapter Six: 'This isn't us' – Jason Bourne, myth and ideology

When Bourne finally limps his way to the Treadstone facility on East 71st Street, Landy is waiting for him. It's quite a sweet moment in the film, the first and only time they meet face to face. Landy, after all, has a particular relationship to the film's protagonist. She nurtures him, in giving him vital information and helping him, all of which makes her an almost maternal figure. Maybe this is how Bourne sees her: as an amnesiac and fugitive, he is after all an orphan. This doesn't mean that Bourne can't indulge in a tiny bit of long-distance flirting with 'Pam', as he calls her: 'You should get some sleep,' he lets her know in the earlier scene, spying on her voyeuristically from across the block; 'You look tired'.

Pam makes up the trinity of female characters – joining Marie and Nicky – who help ease Bourne's passage back into the world toward self-knowledge. It's significant that in the *Bourne* films, the hero goes about his business with virtually no assistance from men. There's no inter-racial 'bromance' here that we find elsewhere in the *Lethal Weapon* (1987–1998) or *Die Hard* (1988–2007) movies; there's no buddying-up with another rogue agent, or blokey get-togethers with special gadget designers. Bourne, in short, is very much a ladies man, though clearly not in the Bond sense: he just seems to trust them more (after Marie is killed at the beginning of *Supremacy*, Bourne is much too busy for sex).

This doesn't necessarily mean that *Ultimatum* totally escapes the overly masculine associations traditionally associated with the action genre. Pam Landy aside, the female characters in the series don't get to do much, besides look scared or concerned. Both Franka Potente and Julia Stiles, who play Marie and Nicky, had their breakthroughs in dynamic, innovative female roles – Potente sprinted her way through the groundbreaking German film *Run Lola Run* (1998), while Stiles combined a sharp tongue with hot moves in *Ten Things I Hate About You* (1999) and *Save the Last Dance* (2001) – but both are relatively subdued in the *Bourne* films, their main function being to provide assistance to the hero (in Film Studies terms they are 'reactive', while Bourne himself is 'active'). While this is a convention, it is not a natural state of affairs: the dominance of women as active protagonists in the horror genre, for example, has been well documented,[42] and recent decades have seen an emergence of the female action heroine in mainstream Hollywood and television (the *Lara Croft: Tomb Raider* films, for instance [2001, 2003], or the recent television show *Nikita* [2010–]), and in the increasingly mainstream action movies of East Asia (*Crouching Tiger, Hidden Dragon* [2000] or *The House of Flying Daggers* [2006]) which in any case have always had strong female roles.

In Hollywood, though, and as the above examples suggest, the female action protagonist tends to be associated with films that are heavily coded as genre films: in other words, not realistic ones. Political assassins and espionage agents do not need to be men, even if they tend to be; but when in films they are women (as in *Nikita*, based on a 1990 French film, *La Femme Nikita*) the assassin's seductive femininity often becomes a key part of the plot, something that makes her a potential threat. For the male assassin, however, seductiveness is merely an asset (the sexual politics of the James Bond series offer an example of this). It would likely need a significant change in representation and association in order for alternative heroes and heroines to be seen in genre movies (though as I suggest in the final chapter, this has possibly begun to take place in the last few years).

Nevertheless, if the *Bourne* series is essentially quite conventional from a gender point of view, there is still room for it to undermine some of the wider associations of masculine representation. Classical Hollywood narration, maintained in many contemporary movies, frequently inter-connects the male protagonist's 'social' goal with the 'private' one – saving the world and winning the girl, to borrow the example of *Transformers* – therefore associating public heroism with heterosexual success. A key difference between the first *Bourne* film and the subsequent ones is that *Identity*'s conclusion, in which a beaming white-shirted Jason turns up at Marie's beachfront restaurant, brings Bourne and Marie together in such a way as to make Bourne 'normal' again. In the Greengrass sequels, this is not an option, and only partly because Marie dies early on. This Bourne only wears black, and never smiles. The emphasis here, in fact, is that Bourne cannot find proper resolution for his actions, and therefore *can never be happy*. Arguably, this makes him merely another kind of hero, a sort of sacrificial one; yet as much as the film allies its protagonist with its series of helpful women, it is also keen to suggest that he comes from a world of highly unappealing men: a world from which he cannot so easily distance himself.

This comes into play at the end of the film, and the appearance of Dr Albert Hirsch. Hirsch, it must be said, is quite easy to forget, though he remains a vital character in the series. Hirsch only appears in the third film, and even then very briefly, aside from his fleeting appearance in Bourne's queasy bleached-out flashbacks. We first see him in the flesh when Vosen calls him, to let him know about Bourne's newly acquired knowledge and imminent appearance. 'He's coming home, Noah', replies Hirsch in a gravelly voice. In keeping with Hollywood tradition, the ultimate villain is played by a British stage actor, in this case Albert Finney; and there's something quite theatrical about the way Bourne finds Hirsch waiting for him on his arrival in the facility. But then, Hirsch is the final piece in the jigsaw, the person that 'joins the dots', to borrow Ross's earlier phrase; the one that holds the key to Bourne's identity. In this way, Hirsch becomes the only real father figure to Bourne. But as 'Bourne' turns out to be a creation of Hirsch, made from the shell of a man once called David Webb, Hirsch is both father *and* mother. He is in this way a sort of Doctor Frankenstein figure, a scientist seeking to recreate life in his image: an idea suggested by the clinical surroundings that brought 'Jason Bourne' – make that *Born* – to life.

Monstrous men and the maintenance of ideology

The end of the film therefore brings together two related myths from the Western narrative tradition: that of Frankenstein, but also that of Oedipus. Frankenstein's monster, as seen in Mary Shelley's original novel of 1818, is essentially a philosophical, thoughtful creature in search of freedom; which in the case of the novel means destroying the father-figure who brought him into hideous, violent being. The original story of Oedipus, as told in ancient Greek drama by Sophocles, was of a man cursed by past, accidental actions: killing his father and marrying his mother. Sigmund Freud, in his study of infant psychology, used the Oedipus story to describe the (male) child's introduction into adult life: at an early stage in his development, this child learns to feel at once separate from his mother, but also envious and fearful of the father's 'access' to the mother. According to Freud, it is during this phase when the male child desires to 'become' his father, mainly by finding a female substitute for his mother, and thereby entering into 'normal' adult life. This is clearly not a plot description for Greengrass's film, yet there are similarities at a certain level. Bourne's loss of memory and identity, as we have seen, make him a kind of child (the opening of *Identity*, like the close of *Ultimatum* in fact, sees him floating in water; a kind of symbolic amniotic fluid suggesting entry into life). He is connected to various surrogate mothers, all of whom are themselves connected to or threatened by the 'father', in the form of the very male-dominated CIA, with its three Big Fathers: Vosen, Ezra Kramer, and Hirsch. And what else is Bourne's motivation in the series but to have a proper identity: in other words, to be a normal person once more in normal, everyday life? In fact, the story of the (male) protagonist battling adversity to find his place in the world is such a staple of popular cinema that it has come to be known as the 'Oedipal narrative' or 'Oedipal trajectory'.[43]

Critics of this type of story suggest that, besides its masculine bias, it tends to express a particular *ideology*. Ideology most superficially describes a way of thinking, but there is a more complex level at which ideology is not what we think, but *what we don't think*. All stable societies have a fairly agreed set of belief systems, even if they don't actively discuss them. When we talk about belief systems, it is often to describe what we think *other* societies think, without stopping to wonder what we believe in, or how or why we might think differently from others. Ideology is tricky, in fact, because by its very nature it makes itself feel natural and unquestioned. As Richard Maltby suggests, it is not 'a specific *list* of beliefs': most of us like to think we're free to choose how we live, so we'd probably want to rebel against such a list. Ideology is, then, 'a *process* by which beliefs... become and continue to be seen as natural, normal, conventional, to such an extent that they are not really seen at all'.[44]

For many analysts of cinema, genre films are effective at maintaining certain beliefs, or at least not challenging them, because of the way they appeal to fantasy, or promote an alternate kind of universe. As Rick Altman argues, genre films are types of ritual or myth, in which the contradictions of society are resolved in an imaginary way. The Western, then, becomes a genre that expresses both the desire for freedom and the need for community; one that celebrates the land at the same time as modern urban expansion is building over it.[45] Or as Geoff King suggests in the case of the action movie, its explosive energy and freedoms provide a compensatory world for otherwise exhausted, rule-abiding viewers; offering 'abundance' and 'intensity' in the place of 'scarcity' and 'dullness'.[46] The possible criticism of this imaginary resolution or compensatory function, which both Altman and King point out, is that these effects offer a kind of pleasurable closure which stops us from questioning things; such as why it is we're all exhausted and rule-abiding to begin with, or why it is we watch Hollywood movies and not documentaries about world poverty (it is, of course, possible to watch both; box-office statistics nevertheless suggest that, for the most part, people tend to watch more of the former).

Movies, then, are often seen as effective instruments of ideology, not when they actively talk about things, but when they actively don't. It's precisely when they are 'just entertainment' that they are most ideological, not on account of what they show, but of what they conceal or exclude.[47] As I've discussed throughout this book, *The Bourne Ultimatum* is positioned doubly as an action-thriller *and* a political drama. As a genre film with a strongly Oedipal protagonist it might be thought to offer simple ideological resolutions; while as a big-budget Hollywood movie, it needs to attract a Friday-night audience. Yet as a film that is grounded in contemporary events, and with a hero who is targeting the actual manufacturers of public beliefs and fears, *Ultimatum* clearly wants to make the workings of ideology more visible. How, if at all, does it manage to do this?

As we saw in Chapter Two, among Greengrass's inspirations in making Ultimatum were American political thrillers of the 1970s, such as *All the President's Men*. Films like these have to perform an ideological balancing act. On the one hand, they have to indicate the evils of America (in the case of *President's Men*, Nixon's administration and the Watergate affair), while at the same time, they have to show that America is good, because it can bring these evils to light and then make movies about them. In the case of *Ultimatum*, the ideological complexity stems from the fact that Bourne and Landy are working to expose the very thing they are part of. This possible contradiction is dealt with by appealing to an idea of non-responsibility. Take for example the scene in which Bourne meets Landy. Bourne reminds Landy that she could be killed for what she's doing. Landy replies that she feels duty-bound to help him. 'This isn't us', she tells him. 'This isn't what I signed up for'. When Landy says that 'this' is not 'us' (which, in turn, also means 'US', as in United States), she is putting herself apart from those elements which don't conform to the desirable view: Vosen, Kramer and Hirsch. In this case, 'us' (or US) becomes her and Bourne: the characters we root for in the film. Her next line is interesting, though. When she says that 'this isn't what I signed up for', we might be forgiven for thinking that she didn't sign up *at all*. But unless the CIA has resorted to press-ganging its senior employees, this is hardly likely. Rather, Landy's siding against the undesirables in this instance allows us, potentially, to forget that she nonetheless remains a loyal servant to the state, not a rebel. At some level, Hollywood's political movies tend to implicitly support the system, or an idea of it, even when they are apparently critical of it.

Role Reversals

We can apply the same logic to Bourne himself. As we know, if Bourne kills in the series it is only because he has no choice: kill or be killed. His personal morality is contrasted with the ruthlessness of the Treadstone/ Blackbriar bosses and the 'assets' who work for them. The attractiveness of Bourne's character, combined with the rush towards narrative resolution he carries with him, means we may forget that Bourne was not an innocent pen-pusher but a political assassin. As we see in the climactic face-off with Hirsch, the film is keen to suggest the kind of brainwashing regime employed to break down David Webb's resistance and turn him into Hirsch's creation, the soulless killing-machine called Jason Bourne. Bourne indicates to Hirsch that, having recovered his memory, and with it the knowledge of becoming Bourne, he is David Webb once again. Hirsch asks Bourne if this means he will now kill him. 'You don't deserve the star they'd give you on the wall at Langley', replies Bourne, alluding here to an honour accorded to CIA men who die in the line of duty.

This pay-off is perhaps too easy; especially in light of the rest of the scene. At the same time, the revelations of this showdown with Hirsch provide the film with greater complexity and interest. The staging of the main flashback sequence, prompted here by Hirsch's words, is a crucial sequence in the context of the series. We see Bourne – or rather Webb – on a chair, with Hirsch demanding he overcome his indecision and commit to the 'programme' (Fig 28). Webb is asking about an unknown man, wanting to know who he is and what he has done. A potential assassination target, perhaps? Hirsch reveals nothing, merely stressing that the programme will help save lives. This stalemate endures for several seconds more, until Webb suddenly rises, a gun drawn in his hand, and aims. Almost too quickly to register, we cut to Webb's point of view, revealing a hooded figure tied to a chair in the corner of the room (Fig 29). Webb unloads the gun into the man's body: the man is then unmasked and acknowledged as dead by a man we recognise as Neal Daniels. The reason for the man's death, or even his identity, remains a mystery.

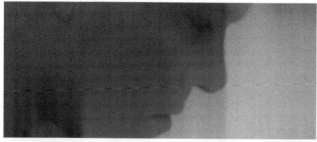

Fig 28: Captain Webb ponders whether to commit...

Fig 29: ... then shoots an unnamed prisoner, watched by Hirsch.

This sequence is clearly meant to shock. Hooded political prisoners and executions, as John Patterson notes in the quotation that opens this book, usually make up the kind of blurry nightmare images retrieved from war zones, and which filter down into the evening news and the press. In the context of the film, this shock is compounded by the fact that it's Bourne who carries out the execution. In truth, it's merely a reminder of what we already knew Bourne to be, yet it's typical within this politically conscientious film that we should be reminded of the fact so brutally at its climax, at a point where (in some other movie, perhaps) revenge might all too easily close off this problematic area of the story.

This aspect of the film also highlights its particular take on the politics of film stardom: an area of the film that so far we have left unexplored, but which cannot be overlooked in our reading of the film. For some writers on cinema, star performance and politics becomes complicated when the star, whose personality precedes the film and is part of its selling power, becomes the message rather than the messenger; in other words, when the star's appeal – which of course defines them as a star – outweighs whatever meanings are at work in the film itself.[48] This, Maltby argues, is the case in the conclusion to *All the President's Men*, where the film's producer and star, Robert Redford (like Damon, a handsome leading man active in left-leaning politics), playing the journalist Bob Woodward, is seen to tidy up what in reality is a much more complex case. In this instance, the documentary-like attention of the film to its subject 'succumbs to the industrial logic of the star system',[49] resolving the film neatly and making Woodward, or rather Redford, the hero of the film.

Maltby may overstate the case here slightly, even if the point is a fair one; yet more significantly, his argument does not account for the way Redford's presence in the film, along with his stardom, is inseparable from his political persona and activism. For Michael Ryan and Douglas Kellner, whose work on the conspiracy film I referred to in the footnotes to Chapter One, the conspiracy movie works best when it allows the audience to empathise with a central figure, an individual: what is a regrettable compromise for Maltby is therefore, for Ryan and Kellner, a means of maintaining humanity within the dehumanising atmosphere of systemic corruption.[50] In this sense, Redford's persona might not be a distraction from the film's meaning, but an integral part of it. It's just that the real meaning of the film is no longer the truth of the Watergate scandal, but rather the long-term desire for institutional change.

We've seen already that *Ultimatum* works partly against the boyish, wholesome image Damon exploited in the early stages of his career (and at the end of *Identity*), though we can also suggest that his *Bourne* persona – the role that has more or less defined his career since 2002, and the series which is effectively defined by his presence – both feeds off and into his star persona, of which his widely reported political views make up a part.[51] As distinct from the everyman heroism of *All the*

President's Men, or any number of other Hollywood movies, the resolution of Bourne's story is quite downbeat, forcing us to see the character in a clearer, more critical light, which does not make so many concessions to the desirability of the star actor. Damon's performance in the series as a whole, in fact, is all about hard work, emphasised by the physicality of his role. In reality, we presume, Damon lives a very comfortable life, with his wife, children and huge fortune. For this reason, it's vital that the star-as-character should at least *appear* to suffer if we are to take his film seriously; and it's for this reason that Bourne has to be dragged through the mud a bit at the end, both spiritually (the memory of the shooting) and physically (getting dumped in the river, as we shall shortly see). It's also a simple reminder that the kind of change and redemption sought after by Bourne is not easily bought – just as real-life political change is not easily won.

The revelation at the end of *Ultimatum* actually returns to the original tale of Oedipus, rather than the Oedipal narrative, albeit with a slight difference. The Oedipal narrative is about the triumphant overcoming of adversity: in the case of *Ultimatum*, this might be the defiance of Hirsch and the film's patriarchal figures. But in the Sophocles play, the story is completely different. *Oedipus the King* starts with a man trying to solve a mystery: why Thebes has been cursed with a plague. Someone must be responsible for bringing this curse upon the city, so Oedipus sets out to find out who it is. The twist is that the detective solves the mystery, only to realise that he is the criminal. The *Bourne* series of novels and films, as we know, works in a similar way. The twist – what the philosopher Aristotle, in his analysis of *Oedipus*, called the 'reversal' – is not as extreme in *Ultimatum* as it is in Sophocles' play, but it's there all the same. It's also been reinforced by Hirsch's statement of Bourne's complicity in the original training: 'Nobody made you do it,' he says. 'You *volunteered*.'

Bourne's previously quoted response deflects much of the responsibility onto Hirsch; just as Frankenstein's monster transfers his own terrible nature onto his creator's actions. Oedipus, by contrast, faces up to his crimes, stabbing hairpins into his eyes and walking off blind into the desert. Oedipus's actions are understandable, but also remarkable: at the time, he had no idea that the man he once killed in self-defence was his father, or that the woman he took as his wife was his mother.

Bourne's amnesia cannot be a defence for this murder, even if it has helped maintain the idea (or illusion) of his innocence over the course of the series. If we choose to disregard this aspect of the film altogether, doesn't that make us responsible for wanting to keep awkward truths under wraps – exactly, in fact, what Vosen, Kramer and Hirsch spend the film trying to do?

If, like Bourne, we experience the revelation as a shock, it is also a neat reminder about the problem of believing what you see. This is the moment of 'recognition' that Aristotle saw as accompanying revelation. As we saw in Chapter Three, *Ultimatum* is largely about looking at things and processing information. At the end, though, there is a blind spot that needs to be filled in from outside, and from the one place neither Bourne nor us can see: the past. The identity that is the object of Bourne's search may not matter as much as the unknown people he tracked down and hunted, the same way that he himself is made to feel tracked and hunted. The film at this point seems to suggest that we balance our empathy for the protagonist with empathy for his victims, and therefore extends to the overall narrative the same type of abrupt, reflective rhythm we have seen in the fight sequences: just at the point we might revel in the hero's victory, we are obliged to look back on its consequences.

Bourne is an action hero, however, not a tragic one. He did a bad thing once – several times, in fact – even if he was no longer 'himself'; but the series doesn't need its hero's sacrifice. It cannot expect its protagonist, like Oedipus, to bend to the power of the Gods, because in this world the Gods that exercise power are those men (and it usually is men, not women) who make the decisions that affect our everyday lives; those who watch our every move, or who send us to wars for reasons we know little about. Bourne's sacrifice would imply that he is the problem. In reality he's a product of the problem: but also, through his efforts, a possible solution.

Weapon Malfunctions

If the now partly restored David Webb rejects responsibility for actions committed as 'Jason Bourne', even if he volunteered for Hirsch's programme, the film strongly implies that the programme was based on a lie. The film also hints that the real subject is not one assassin, but the programme (in the real world, perhaps, the American and coalition-led 'War on Terror') in its entirety. David Webb, we find out, was actually Captain Webb – Hirsch has his dog tags – which indicates the military origins of the programme (in the original novels, Webb served in Vietnam). Webb volunteers, it seems, not because he is a gun-happy sociopath, but because he believes what he is told: that, in Hirsch's words, he will be 'saving American lives'. Anyone vaguely familiar with the type of language associated since the 9/11 attacks with the 'War on Terror' – not just the work of global intelligence, but also the military interventions in Afghanistan and Iraq – will recognise this kind of language. But anyone familiar with the unresolved nature of this war will also know how dangerously indiscriminate such language can be. The invasion of Iraq, led predominantly by the US and Britain under what is believed by many to be false pretences (the presence of non-existent WMD, or Weapons of Mass Destruction), along with its lingering aftermath, can be seen as embodying the possible wastes of this war, which has cost the lives of thousands of soldiers, and an equal (perhaps even greater) number of civilians.

Ultimatum, released in the recent memory of both 9/11 and London's 7 July 2007 (7/7) attacks, and during the fourth year of the drawn-out Iraq war, is well aware of the uneasy nature of living with the threat of terrorism; but it is also aware of the danger of paranoia, and the long-term damage of making everyone a possible enemy. The ironic twist on this in the film is that Bourne, once back in New York, becomes for Vosen's crew a top priority terrorist threat. It's this crew that are after Bourne now, bearing down on him seconds after the key revelation, and forcing Bourne to run again. Bourne makes for the roof, only to find himself trapped: on one side, by those who want him dead, on the other, by a long drop into the water. Bourne's options are further limited by the reappearance of Paz, who has freed himself from the crash where Bourne left him and resumed his pursuit. His weapon trained on Bourne, Paz speaks: the only time, in fact, we hear either him or Desh utter a word in the whole film, a detail which underscores their machine-like nature. 'Why didn't you take the shot?' he asks, sounding almost disappointed not to be dead. 'You don't even know why you're supposed to kill me', replies Bourne wearily. 'Look at us. Look at what they make you give'. A noise offscreen alerts us to the presence of the other pursuers, and the shadowy figure of Vosen steps out of a doorway. Bourne leaps: as he does so, we see Paz lower his gun, then Vosen fire. From afar, Bourne is seen falling into the East River, before an underwater shot shows his body entering the water. Calmness finally descends on the film, with a long shot of the river and the lights of the city in the distance.

Bourne's last words to Paz echo his own despair at a wasted life in the service of an empty idea. It's actually the same line uttered in *The Bourne Identity* by 'The Professor' – one of the Treadstone ops sent throughout Europe to take out Bourne – as he lies dying in a French field from Bourne's gunshot wound. Echoing The Professor's words here gives circularity and symmetry to the action, but also a kind of finality. But the role-reversal also turns Paz, effectively, into Bourne: the killer turned questioner. Like Bourne, Paz has been asked to kill on order, without explanation. Once again, the film shows its allegiances with the loyal but misinformed servants. The masters, it suggests, are the monsters.

Bourne, ultimately more of an anti-hero than a conventional hero, has done terrible things; but it is perhaps the recognition of these terrible acts that makes his return back to David Webb more valid. He can choose a different path, rather than accept his fate as a monster. It's also a recognition that should be shared by us as viewers. If we want to see the film within the context of recent political events, it is important to place the protagonist within, and not outside, the area of moral uncertainty, especially if the efforts to redeem and rebuild are to mean anything at all. The anti-hero's endurance also offers both the hope and thrill of combating all those forces mobilised against him – and, if we believe it, against us. Bourne as an avenging moral monster is an exciting one because, as we saw in the Waterloo sequence and the film's various chase sequences, he turns against his creators all the training and skills they have given him. It might be Bourne's seriously damaged nature, in fact, that makes him best suited to turn the tables and redress balances, converting him basically into a malfunctioning military asset. A weird kind of hero, then, for a world in which nothing is quite what it seems.

Footnotes

42. In, for example, Carol Clover, *Men, Women and Chainsaws: Gender in the Modern Horror Film* (London: BFI, 1992).

43. Susan Hayward, *Cinema Studies: the Key Concepts* (London and New York: Routledge, 2000), pp. 261–262.

44. Maltby, *Hollywood Cinema*, p. 302.

45. Rick Altman, 'Cinema and Genre', in Geoffrey Nowell-Smith (ed), *The Oxford Guide to World Cinema* (Oxford and New York: Oxford University Press, 1996), pp. 276–285 (p. 285).

46. King, *Spectacular Narratives*, p. 103.

47. Maltby, *op cit.*, p. 300.

48. The first major academic work in English to consider the meaning of stardom, and still the most influential, is Richard Dyer's *Stars* (London: BFI, 1979).

49. Maltby, *op cit.*, p. 388.

50. Ryan and Kellner, *Camera Politica*, pp. 99–100.

51. In the publicity around *Ultimatum*, Damon was frequently quoted as saying that the film was resonant with contemporary events and the US's war in Iraq in particular. In 2008, Damon was an active supporter of Barack Obama's presidential campaign, but more recently has become his most high-profile Democrat critic (see for example Tom Teodorczuk, 'From No 1 fan to critic-in-chief, Damon takes aim at Obama', *The Independent on Sunday*, 6 March 2011).

Summary and questions

- *The Bourne Ultimatum* draws on narrative myths such as Frankenstein and Oedipus as structures that underpin its story. These myths have certain functions in cinema, enabling us to identify with or understand protagonists' narrative trajectories, or even accept certain ideas (ideologies).

- The film's resolution is complex, because its satisfaction of narrative trajectory overlooks Bourne's possible responsibility. The revelation of Bourne's beginnings raises questions about his innocence.

- The ambiguity around Bourne, possibly, is intended to underline the importance of choice: in this case, Bourne's rejection of his past life. The film suggests an analogy between government actions and the misplaced trust these actions have generated.

- Bourne's actions overturn the rule of authority: he uses his given skills against his masters, not for them.

- Is the moral ambiguity something you notice when watching the *Bourne* movies?

- What is the appeal in contemporary cinema of protagonists going against orders?

- How many other recent movies use similar myths as part of their narrative? What is the enduring appeal of these mythic stories?

Chapter Seven: Cue the Music – *Bourne* and Serial Cinema

After the face-off with Paz and Vosen, which ends with Webb tumbling into New York's East River, there is an abrupt change of pace. A leap forward in time shows us Landy beginning to give her testimony at a Congressional Hearing into the Treadstone and Blackbriar programmes. At the same time, a shot of the now black-bobbed Nicky Parsons, drinking a beer in an unspecified bar, shows her watching the breaking news on TV: the arrest of Hirsch, Kramer and Vosen (the 'real' has become a news story in the end). The reporter then mentions the unknown fate of David Webb, the identity of 'Jason Bourne' now openly displayed on television screens. Nicky looks on anxiously; her face then records the moment of recognition and pleasure, as the newscast reveals that Webb's body, following a three-day search of the river, was not found.

If we're still with the film at this point, and if we're still with the series after five and a half hours and thousands of miles of action, then Nicky's knowing smile is also ours. If we wanted to be picky about it, we might throw our hands up at this point and shout out a big '*as if!*' If Paz *really* would have let him go, and if Vosen's shot *really* didn't kill him, then surely a sixty-foot fall into the freezing river might have finished the job. But no! As the camera lingers on Parsons' face, we hear the siren-like opening bursts of Moby's song 'Strange Ways': cut back to the floating body, which, as if prompted by the music, pulses into life and swims away into the murky water. Fade to black; roll the end credits.

The more probable ending is not always desirable in cinema: if it were, the history of the medium would be very different. In any case, the ending of *The Bourne Ultimatum* is actually rather subtle. While we're told that Webb's body was not recovered, this suggests no more than what it says: the gap is filled by Nicky and the viewer, willing the hero back to life. Even the shot of a Webb-like figure swimming away, placed as it is after the shot of Nicky, is ambiguous in its murky lack of clarity: is this *really* Webb, or is it merely Webb as imagined by Nicky?

I'm not sure it matters, and in any case we can't really say. *Ultimatum* ends like this simply because that is how it has to be: the genre, and more importantly the series, demands it. Bourne has to endure, and promise to return – even if, as we'll see in the next chapter, he may not. But it also adds to the overall feel and impact of the film(s). It's like that great moment at the end of early *24* seasons when, the dust having settled on one attempted atrocity, a new crisis begins and the clock, for the first and only time, clicks down to zero, back to the beginning. We love it because it suggests duration, and a life beyond the running time of one film or one season. The show goes on: come back later for more.

Play it Again (and Again)

The use of Moby's song is effective here because it's the same song used for the previous two films, and fans of the series will recognise it instantly as the end music. This is not in itself anything new – the *Star Wars* films, to give the most obvious example, always end with the same burst of John Williams' score. Yet the use of a pop song (one that wasn't written specifically for the film) to provide coherence and familiarity throughout the series is notable: unlike the Williams score in *Star Wars*, it suggests a cool, contemporary feel that we associate more with television than with cinema. Despite their primary existence and format as big screen entertainment (*Ultimatum* is shot in 2.40:1 anamorphic widescreen, the most television-unfriendly screen ratio), there is a very televisual quality of repetition and familiarity evoked by the series. This episodic quality to the *Bourne* films is something it shares with other film series, for example the *Mission: Impossible* films (1996–), which are themselves adapted from a popular 1960s TV show (CBS, 1966–1973).

Whatever connections exist between film and television, which I'll consider below, it's important to think about the differing connotations of a 'series' across the different media. Throughout this book I've used this televisual word to describe the *Bourne* films, rather than the more familiar cinematic term of 'franchise'. Does it matter what we call it? Many would argue that it does. The word 'franchise', connected as it is with the term 'blockbuster' is for some a bit of a dirty word. This is because its origins have little connection with art and more to do with business: technically, it refers to the legal ownership and the right to make money from particular goods or services. With reference to modern Hollywood, the term is typically associated with what we call intellectual or entertainment properties, or just 'properties' for short. In cinema terms, a property can be a title or character, or group of characters, an invented world or a story. Films linked by a coherent and usually pre-existing serial narrative (*Harry Potter* [2001–2011], *Lord of the Rings* [2001–2003], both of which we might legitimately call series) are types of franchises, but the best examples are those films linked less by a serial narrative, than by an overarching concept or character. In the case of Disney's *Pirates of the Caribbean* films (2003–), for example, there is no original narrative from which the films are adapted: as is well known, the original inspiration for the series is a ride at Disneyland. Superhero characters, meanwhile, are the properties of the comic companies who invented them: DC's Batman and Superman; Spider-Man, Iron Man, Hulk and so on at Marvel, who recently set up their own film production division to maintain greater control over their creations' cinematic outings.

For those sceptical about such things, franchises, and the sequels that perpetuate them, are an example of what Hollywood does worst. Because their impact is based largely on repetition around established formulae, they can be seen as – and often are – unimaginative films whose primary function is to make money for the companies that produce them. Sequels, suggests film historian Kristin Thompson, 'usually are seen as an attempt to milk the success of one film by making a second that will probably not live up to the original's quality and success'.[52] Maltby suggests that the franchise is economically important to studios for two further reasons. Firstly, franchises make up a key part of a studio's film 'library', which creates assets for the company through DVD/Blu-Ray units and sales to television; secondly, they generate a brand recognition that is marketable beyond the film itself, in the form of merchandising, and especially videogame tie-ins.[53] This economic criticism of franchises is often connected to the fact that the companies involved in film production and distribution, most of which already have interests beyond film, are now part of a wider network of global corporations that are all seeking to extend their brands through collaboration. In film-industry jargon, this is known as creating 'synergy'.[54]

It's reasonable to be cynical about the way global conglomerates dominate and control what is termed, uncomfortably but correctly, the 'entertainment industry'. But are the arguments against the blockbuster franchise overstated? From its earliest days Hollywood was always about making a buck, but the best way to do this usually was, and to a reasonable extent still is, to make the best product possible. The *Godfather* films, the first two parts in particular (1970 and 1972), were big productions that made lots of money for their producers (Paramount). They were based originally on a best-selling novel that, like the *Bourne* books, was never in line for highbrow literary awards. Both *Godfather* films nevertheless won Best Picture Academy Awards and regularly feature in critics' lists of all-time great movies. Yet in principle we should be as cynical about *The Godfather Part Two* as we might be about *The Return of the King* (2003) or *The Dark Knight*; films which in theory (as franchise movies) represent what is 'bad' about contemporary cinema, but also (as fine pieces of popular art) much that is great about them.[55]

The problem with thinking about sequels only in terms of profits is that, as an argument, it overlooks how audiences respond to them. As the examples of the *Godfather*, *Batman* and *Rings* movies suggest, there may be more to the sequel and the franchise than mere repetition. Film series, in other words, have significant qualities as a group of individual films, but they are also interesting – we might even say more interesting – when taken together *as a series*. Discussing the *Godfather* films, of which there are now three (the third instalment appeared in 1990), Thompson suggests that there is a point at which we start seeing sequels as a series, which for her is not just a question of definition, but a different way of seeing the films.[56] The motivation behind *The Godfather: Part Two* may at some level have been to 'cash in' on the success of the first film, yet the sequel did not simply carry on where the original left off, but instead, introduced a pre-story that traced the origins of 'Godfather' Vito Corleone's family in the immigrant communities of early twentieth-century America. The result was not only a film which many thought richer and more accomplished than the first, but the expansion of *The Godfather* as a film into a layered and complex fictional 'saga'. It's in this sense that the *Godfather* films take on the qualities of modern American history, way beyond their status as fiction films; qualities that one movie, however unique, would be less likely to have.

Worldmaking

We've already seen that *The Bourne Ultimatum* begins by putting us in the middle of the action, with Bourne on the run from the Moscow police. Opening a film like this – what literary theory calls starting *in media res*, literally 'in the middle of things' – is not in itself that radical; in fact it's quite common in thrillers or detective films, not to mention many of Shakespeare's plays. The difference is that, whereas the opening incident is usually what the film's action proceeds from, or that which the rest of the film tries to make sense of, the opening action in *Ultimatum* has nothing to do with what happens in the rest of the film. Someone new to the series, watching the third film first, might not worry too much about this. But it would leave a largely unanswered question throughout the film's opening scenes, which would require going back to *Identity* and *Supremacy* in order to resolve.

Extending the narrative across three instalments means that the viewer can go back and forth in this way, visiting or revisiting the different episodes of the series in order to make sense of the whole story. Working through three films rather than one also affords the storytelling more time and space, therefore allowing more complexity and detail. As we've seen, the Bourne narrative is in essence a very simple one (Who am I?), but it is one made richer by the questions that follow (What did I do? Why did I do it? What can I do to atone for it?). As some reviewers of the film suggested, in terms of action and structure, *Ultimatum* was an upgraded rehash of *Supremacy*, but this is less important than the way in which the third film brings together the narrative threads that have been in play since the beginning of the series. The beauty of multiple-part continuous narratives like this, then, is that they *accumulate* interest and expectation as they go on, rather than drag out an increasingly tired idea like other non-continuous franchises (which, needing to constantly reinvent themselves, and always in danger of becoming predictable, tend to get progressively worse from sequel to sequel). This may explain why, unusually for a second sequel, *Ultimatum* was more popular than the first two films.

Giving time and space to a film series also lets its parts breathe, giving them a weight of development and resolution. In the case of the *Bourne* films, it also allows space for the more political aspects of the series to be explored alongside the central story. We might imagine a more hectic version of the three films condensed into one, *Mission: Impossible* style, with Bourne going from Switzerland to New York via Moscow in the space of two hours. This might be fun, but the detail accumulated in the three-film series – Bourne's development, the Treadstone and Blackbriar programmes, the role of US intelligence, the various characters and the parts they play – would be surrendered in favour of the single overarching narrative. In this case, Bourne/Webb's revelation in New York would have no impact, because there would be too little context for us to care about it. Maybe it's for this reason that many one-off action-thrillers need to end with fights or explosions for them to feel satisfying, but why both *Supremacy* and *Ultimatum* can be rounded off in a relatively understated fashion.

Series such as the *Bourne* films, therefore, exploit, like all the best series, what Bordwell calls 'worldmaking': the desire to create in the film 'a rich, fully furnished ambience for the action'.[57] Seriality extends the space and length of narrative, allowing us to inhabit it and grow familiar with it: a space in which characters and events refer to one another and interconnect. Repetition and recurrence make the difference between a set of random events and a wider, coherent sense of time, space and action. Hollywood franchises, it's important to point out, did not invent this. Its immediate forerunners are found in nineteenth-century literature: writers like Dickens in England and Balzac in France, whose novels, like modern-day comics, were originally published as magazine-style serials before being collected into book form. Until the emergence of film and television, whose own narrative forms it inspired, the great urban novel was arguably the dominant cultural medium of its age. Its popularity offers an indication of the long-standing desire for these 'fully furnished' fictional worlds, but it's also a good example of the way consumer desire and capitalist interest can actually shape media forms (in this instance, for the good).

If there were only a *Bourne Identity*, and no other films, we would have an example of an extremely competent thriller, but no sense of the complex narrative and environment the three movies (and originally, the novels) provide. Both the *Bourne* films and Dickens' novels are, of course, fictional: yet because of their extended serial nature they do not feel fictional, but rather assume the quality of real life. There are wider implications here, too. The fictional nature of the nineteenth-century novel has not prevented its being seen as a form of social and historical document. Many readers look to *Bleak House* (1852–53) or *Little Dorrit* (1855–57) for a window on the world of London in the mid-1800s, in spite of the fact that the plots themselves are pure invention. But then, that's not exactly true: just as Greengrass uses a detailed, documentary-like approach in his movies, Dickens used a journalistic approach in his novels to capture a sense of his world, realised through representative characters and spaces: his novels, in short, are an example of fiction being used to imaginatively convey fact. As I've suggested, the *Bourne* films do exactly the same on film: everything we see in *Ultimatum* is made up for the camera, yet its locations are real, its references have real-world implications, and its events *could* happen.

Big Small Screens

It's also important, finally, to recognise the significance of television and its relationship to the big screen in the twenty-first century; not merely because it was in the medium of television that *Ultimatum*'s director learnt his craft. The distinctions between cinema and television were once clear-cut: movies were seen at the cinema, and later, depending on the whims of programming, on television. Television, meanwhile, which became a dominant household object from the 1950s, made shows that were at best mini-versions of theatrical films. At a later point, television drama began to make up for its more limited screen size by extending its narrative breadth. In the 1980s and 1990s, cop shows like *Hill Street Blues* (NBC, 1981–1987) and *NYPD Blue* (ABC, 1993–2005), along with the long-running hospital drama *ER* (NBC, 1994–2009), moved away from the self-contained episode format of much television, spinning out bigger narratives – known in the industry as 'A plots' – over the space of several episodes, a whole series, as in *24*, or even multiple series: the six seasons of *Lost* (ABC, 2004–2010), for example, effectively constitute one overarching story.

These series maintain their complexity and interest, and therefore their longevity, by interweaving 'B', 'C' and 'D' plots (and so on) into the 'A' plot.[58] We can apply this pattern to the *Bourne* films. *Identity* sets up the A plot – Who is Jason Bourne? – that will sustain the narrative across the three films. *Supremacy* continues this A plot, but introduces B and C plots: Bourne's search for Marie's killer, and for the orphaned girl in Moscow. These secondary plots work as self-contained storylines, which enables *Supremacy* to work as a stand-alone episode, but significantly, they also help to develop the A plot. Marie's death is a catalyst that sets Bourne firmly back on the trail; just as the search for the Russian girl opens up new areas of Bourne's memory and brings him closer to his overall goal. *Ultimatum*, meanwhile, introduces a new character and storyline – Simon Ross and Blackbriar – which again allows the film to work as a self-contained episode, but which also works to bring together the final narrative paths.

More than narrative breadth, modern television has also achieved a level of detail and complexity that the one-off feature film, frankly, cannot imagine within its limited time frame. Dramas like *The West Wing* (NBC, 1999–2006) *The Sopranos* (HBO, 1999–2007), and above all *The Wire* (HBO, 2002–2008), have altered the conception of serial drama as an 'entertainment' medium. Shows like the last two mentioned above, because they are produced by a subscription channel (Home Box Office) and are not, therefore, at the mercy of network-imposed restrictions on bad language and the depiction of sex and violence, also have more freedom in terms of content and formats. One of the results of this has been what we might call 'smart' television: series whose elaborate, multi-narrative forms do not give the viewer everything on a plate, but demand that the viewer watches and listens closely, making links and deductions across the time and space of the series as a whole.

Much media theory has argued that such attention on the part of viewers was the property of films, not television: films, according to this argument, were the subject of an intensive 'gaze', while television – once a flickering box in the corner of the room – was the object of a 'glance'.[59] The recent examples suggest, though, that the balance is shifting. It is true that over the same period we have seen an increasingly 'smart' streak in Hollywood film production: think about the narrative games played by films such as *The Usual Suspects* (1995) or *Memento* (2000),[60] or sprawling multi-character films like *Magnolia* (1999); films which Bordwell describes as 'network' narratives.[61] Yet it is above all the complexity and social detail of television series which, I would argue, provide the inspiration for a series such as the *Bourne* films: both in the films' efforts to create a plausible world for the action, and in the demands it places on viewers to absorb and process information at pace.

Footnotes

52. Kristin Thompson, *Storytelling in Film and Television* (Cambridge and London: Harvard University Press, 2003), pp. 98–99.

53. Maltby, *Hollywood Cinema*, pp. 205–208.

54. Maltby, *ibid.*, pp. 208–209.

55. For an extended argument along these lines, see Tom Shone, *Blockbuster: How the Jaws and Jedi Generation Turned Hollywood into a Boom-Town* (London: Simon and Schuster, 2004).

56. Thompson, *Storytelling*, p. 100.

57. Bordwell, *The Way Hollywood Tells It*, pp. 58–59.

58. Thompson, *op cit.*, p. 31.

59. This argument is outlined in John Ellis, *Visible Fictions* (London and New York: Routledge and Kegan Paul, 1982).

60. See Warren Buckland (ed.), *Puzzle Films: Complex Storytelling in Contemporary Cinema* (Malden and Oxford: Blackwell, 2009).

61. Bordwell, *op cit.*, pp. 98–100.

Summary and questions

- Series or franchises such as the *Bourne* films often have a poor reputation, despite being popular, as they are associated with commercialism: the desire to generate more money through sequels and merchandising tie-ins.

- These economic arguments fail to account for the appeal of serial narratives and cinematic 'worlds' for viewers: greater detail, more subtle narrative and character development, and an interactive relationship to the text(s).

- We can arguably detect a closer relationship between film and television narratives, particularly in terms of how series function.

- In what way do you think the serial nature of much contemporary cinema adds to the experience of films?

- Is *The Bourne Ultimatum* more interesting as a 'complex' narrative, with its origins in other instalments? Does the end of the film make you want to see a continuation of the series?

- How do you find the 'cinematic' experience changes between different viewing platforms? Do you regard watching the *Bourne* films online, on TV or on DVD as a 'cinematic' or 'televisual' experience?

Chapter Eight: The *Bourne* Legacy – Or, What J.B. Did Next

In the time between the release of *The Bourne Ultimatum* and this book being published, a fourth *Bourne* movie saw the light of day. After a long period of pre-production, *The Bourne Legacy*, directed by *Ultimatum* screenwriter Tony Gilroy, reached international cinema screens in August 2012. If you've seen the film you might have noticed that Matt Damon wasn't in it. Or, for that matter, Jason Bourne. All of which begs the question: is this a *Bourne* movie at all? What exactly is *The Bourne Legacy*? And without either J.B. or M.D., what's the point?

Gilroy attempted to address these questions in an interview during the film's production: 'The easiest way to think of it is an expansion or a reveal'.[62] Not quite a prequel or sequel, but rather a kind of 'side-quel': a film exploring aspects of Bourne's world, parallel to the events of *Ultimatum*, focusing on another agent in Bourne's image (Aaron Cross, played by Jeremy Renner), and featuring some of the characters – Ezra Kramer, Noah Vosen, Albert Hirsh – who figured prominently in the earlier film. While some of the staple action sequences, such as car chases and rooftop pursuits, were preserved, Gilroy looked to bring a slightly less frenetic visual style to the series, just as he sought to take the saga in new directions; for example, in the introduction of Marta Shearing (Rachel Weisz), a geneticist involved in the agent training programme, who, like Cross, is also forced to flee for her life.

As a franchise movie, *Legacy* faced a difficult task, one largely forced upon it when both Matt Damon and Paul Greengrass opted out of a fourth outing for the eponymous hero. Perhaps inevitably, the film's reception – both critically, where it received favourable but not ecstatic reviews, and commercially, where it failed to match the impact of the previous two instalments – reflected its status as a kind of 'optional' *Bourne* movie. In truth, the desire to approach the story from a parallel perspective, with the action of *Legacy* overlapping with the events of *Ultimatum*, is an interesting one: less common in movies, it is a familiar practice in the world of comics (especially at Marvel), where multiple titles run simultaneous and frequently inter-weaving storylines. Five years on after *Ultimatum*, though, it might be taxing the good will of its audience to engage with such a concept; yet it remains a smart decision in light of the fact that any saga has its natural point of exhaustion. Despite *Ultimatum*'s open ending, with his identity revealed and his enemies' crimes made public, how much more (literal) mileage could they drag out of Jason Bourne? If we believe Greengrass – who reputedly said that a fourth instalment should be called *The Bourne Redundancy* – not very much.

The ability to generate sequels, often of diminishing quality and interest, is of course not the best indicator of a film's influence within culture. Beyond the *Bourne* franchise itself, what is the afterlife of a film like *Ultimatum*? If the way films are discussed by the media is still meaningful, affecting the way certain styles or types are received and perceived, what is Bourne's legacy? A significant one, apparently. *Empire* magazine's staff writers voted *Ultimatum* their film of 2007 (just as, perhaps more surprisingly, they had voted Greengrass's *United 93* the film of 2006). A more unexpected form of recognition came in the pages of *Sight & Sound*; a magazine that, as I pointed out earlier, tends not to favour big-budget Hollywood films. In a 2010 edition devoted to 'Cinema of the 21st Century', the magazine included Greengrass's movie among their list of thirty films which 'best represent the [first] decade's most distinctive oeuvres and movements' (James, 2010: 36).

Given *Sight & Sound*'s interest in cinematic innovation and distinctive film-making from around the world, the highlighting of *Ultimatum* in this list was significant; especially as it was much more obviously commercial than the other chosen films (the only other American films on the list were Spike Jonze's *Adaptation* (2002) and Paul Thomas Anderson's *There Will Be Blood* (2007): both exceptional, original films, but far from conventional Hollywood movies). As Nick James wrote in the accompanying article, along the lines of the argument I outlined in Chapter Three: 'Despite our professed dislike of Michael Bay-style editing, there is one exception. When that approach is taken to really brutal extremes, as it is in Paul Greengrass's *The Bourne Ultimatum*, we beg leave to contradict ourselves'.[63] James's point is that *Ultimatum* manages to do something with the mainstream movie that is at once innovative and exciting, using the techniques of the action thriller to reflect the post-9/11 anxieties of the modern city. The implication of James's comments, though, is that other genre movies may learn from Bourne's example.

What J.B. Did Next, Part One

We can see this through one very high-profile example. 2008 saw the release of the twenty-second Bond film, *Quantum of Solace*; the second of the series featuring Daniel Craig in the lead role, and a follow-up to 2006's successful Bond 'reboot', *Casino Royale*. The 2006 film, as we touched upon earlier, offered a 'revisionist' vision of Ian Fleming's character: one that was still recognisably Bond, and in some ways even closer to the spirit of the original book. What *Casino Royale* injected into the old franchise were greater doses of physicality, brutality, and speed. These qualities were further upped in *Quantum*; the first film in the Bond franchise not to be based on any of Fleming's fiction, and one that stretched the Bond concept to breaking point. This was a Bond stripped bare of many of the things that defined the franchise in the first place: gone were the gadgets and glossy automobiles, the tailored suits and sexual innuendo. The famous martini returns, but only for a spot of mile-high binge-drinking. This was a hardened Bond for hard times, a lone wolf in a world where the line between good and evil is increasingly blurred.

Any description of *Quantum* ends up sounding, inevitably, like the summary of a *Bourne* movie. Car chases and fights are filmed up close, the camera itself seemingly shaken (*and* stirred) by pounding fists and white-knuckle crashes; elsewhere, we leap with Bond head-on over crumbling rooftops. Like *Ultimatum*, it starts literally at speed, in the middle of a breakneck car pursuit along an unspecified coastal road. Eventually it becomes clear that this is a continuation of the previous film's action: we have picked up where we left off in *Casino Royale*, after the death of Vesper Lind. The new film, without pausing for any recap, throws us straight into Bond's search for revenge, and for the truth behind Vesper's actions. This is '*The Bond Supremacy*', in other words; just as *Casino Royale*, which is partly about how 007 became 007, could be '*The Bond Identity*'. In my ideal world, the next Bond would have been conceived along the lines of '*The Bond Ultimatum*': a film in which Bond, struck by memory loss and blurry flashbacks – maybe of secret-service brainwashing at Cambridge – heads back to England to gun down his old tormentors, then retires to run a cocktail bar with Moneypenny.

It's sometimes been hinted that the Bond films, after *Die Another Day* in 2002, were forced to change due to the success the *Bourne* franchise.

While there is some mileage to this theory, as I'll suggest below, it may somewhat overstate the fact. The idea of making *Quantum* a straight sequel to *Casino Royale* is certainly a break in Bond tradition, though as we saw in the last chapter, multi-instalment narratives have become a dominant concern in the film industry. We've also seen that between Bourne and Bond (not forgetting Bauer) there is mutual influence at work; and in any case, once we start identifying who influences whom, we need to go back from Bourne to Bond himself. The *Bourne* novels, like the films, read like their own take on the world of Bond, and it's hard to imagine things such as the *Bourne* series without the existence of Fleming's agent somewhere in our mental background. We've also seen how much the *Bourne* franchise owes to other cultural texts that run alongside it, including *24*. In the end, which came first is not really the point: the so-called 'Bournification' of Bond is of interest mainly for what it tells us about the style and content of contemporary action thrillers in general.

A key point is that, by the end of the Brosnan Bonds, the series was hardly a dwindling commodity. Contrary to what we might expect, the shift in look and feel of the Bond films between *Die Another Day* and *Quantum of Solace* was not necessarily motivated by economics. Quoting one of the producers behind the Bond franchise, James Chapman argues that Bond's privileged box-office status worldwide meant that series like the *Bourne* films were not genuine competitors in economic terms.[64] Despite the recognition by Bond fans, including Chapman, that *Die Another Day* was one of the weakest films in the series, it still amassed $430 million at the box office (most of which came from markets outside the US, indicating Bond's global appeal), and in the process set new records for the franchise.[65] Why fix something, then, that isn't broken? Chapman's justification for the franchise reboot in *Casino Royale* is that the film wanted to capture the hard-nosed essence of Fleming's novel, rather than follow the contemporary mood for more realist, morally blurred espionage series such as *24*, *Spooks* and the *Bourne* films.[66] While this argument explains the style of *Casino Royale*, and its violence in particular, it doesn't however account for the motive behind this 'back-to-basics' adaptation in the first place; unless it be, in Chapman's words, the desire 'to reinvent [the franchise] by returning to more plausible, if not strictly realistic, narratives'.[67]

Plausibility, though, is a shifting concept, related to the way things are represented in culture. Every era has its plausible or realistic narratives, and these only come to seem implausible in retrospect, due to changes in content and style. The earliest Bond films, such as *Dr No* (1962) (let alone any of those mid-period ones starring Roger Moore) are hard to take seriously now, which is why their style, colours and cartoony villains lend themselves to Austin Powers-style parody. But if audiences in the 1960s thought the Connery Bonds were just camp (a concept, in fact, that hadn't yet entered the mainstream), it's hard to imagine why they would be so popular in the first place; and in fact, as Chapman points out, many critics at the time complained about *Dr No*'s violence and amorality.[68] If never convincingly true-to-life, their pace and action probably seemed more realistic and more hard-edged fifty years ago (as we saw in Chapter Three, *Goldfinger* was a very 'fast' film for its time). But tastes change, as does our idea of what is 'realistic'. It doesn't make sense, then, to disregard the influence of other films on the Bond films, as these other movies contribute to what we understand as realistic or plausible depictions of the world.

A franchise that might happily have continued in the same vein as before – packed with product placement, invisible cars and serial promiscuity – rebooted itself, it seems, not necessarily to make more money, but *to be taken more seriously*. Put slightly differently, the franchise changed because it was out of date. Exactly why, though, was only partly to do with movies.

Like a Movie: Representing Reality after 9/11

The most influential visual event of this century's first decade was not a film or TV show, but the September 11 2001 terror attacks on targets in the United States, and on the World Trade Center in particular: an act that was screened live, recorded, and then replayed from dozens of angles and perspectives on the television news for days afterwards and documentaries ever since.[69] The 9/11 attacks changed the way we see things for two main reasons: firstly, because they seemed to evoke the kind of images of destruction already familiar to us from disaster movies such as *Armageddon* and *Deep Impact* (both 1998), and therefore confused the boundaries of Hollywood fantasy and reality; secondly, because they turned mass death and destruction into a primetime television spectacle.

These images, and of course the events that came in their wake, have seeped into our movies in various ways, even in films superficially very different from the *Bourne* franchise. From a distance, the popular cinema of the twenty-first century appears to celebrate pure escape: a closer look suggests that, at some level, this cinema has a more serious point of reference, if not serious intent. The Bond series' shifting of targets, from Cold War politics to the bankrollers of global terrorism, is possibly an exchange of one stereotype for another, but at least the new films inject elements of moral ambiguity into the series (recall the fact that, early on in *Casino Royale*, Bond shoots dead an unarmed bomb-maker in a foreign embassy).[70] Commentators on American film since 9/11, meanwhile, have stressed the way that even the superhero films directed at the teenage demographic, Christopher Nolan's Batman films in particular, have incorporated 'moral angst [and] adult-level pain', along with hints of 9/11 itself, into what is basically an escapist genre: 'today, the vigilantes in primary-colour tights... don't confront the conjectural fears of the Cold War, but the all too tangible, falling-bodies verities of the new millennium'.[71] Note, for example, how we have moved from the pantomime silliness of Jack Nicholson's Joker in Tim Burton's *Batman* to Heath Ledger's shambling amoral void in *The Dark Knight*; a character quite happy to blow up a hospital or bomb a commuter ferry, in a city that looks like one the audience might actually live in.

Espionage thrillers, meanwhile, if we are to believe them, need to locate their stories in a more credible environment with real-world references. I have shown how *Ultimatum* draws on anxieties about crowded spaces and strangers, in a way that evokes our own present-day fears. But we've also seen how the film engages with the fear of fear itself: the paranoia that pursues without discrimination and risks generating greater division and tension. The subtext now is that the actions of corporations, of our governments and their agencies across the globe, are at once covert and totally transparent: we know everything, even if we can't always say what it is we know. This realisation is characterised, naturally, by a deep pessimism about figures of power and authority in general. For Michael Atkinson, then, a film like *Ultimatum* is 'soaked in a learned cynicism' that makes Vietnam-era films like *All the President's Men*, with its faith in the power of good journalism, 'seem naïve'.[72]

A truer legacy for Bourne may then be the number of films, made in the few years after *Ultimatum*, that have drawn on similar themes and aesthetic qualities; films that have in common a misled or misdirected protagonist at their centre, and that share a deep scepticism towards figures of authority, together with a film-making sensibility honed in places other than Hollywood. In *Salt* (2010), directed by the Australian Philip Noyce, Angelina Jolie plays an American secret service operative who may or may not be a Russian mole, out to initiate a new Cold War by assassinating the reformist Russian president. The film keeps us guessing as to how much its eponymous agent is telling the truth about her situation, or whether she is just covering up, with a great deal of the plot remaining an unfathomable mystery. If the story itself is a throwback to an earlier era of espionage movies, it is notable for the way that, post-Bourne, the emphasis is not on maintaining old political enemies, but tracking down the outdated opponents to political co-operation and diplomacy. Blind spots of memory and the search for identity also come to the fore in *Hanna* (2011), directed by Joe Wright (the British director of *Pride and Prejudice* [2005] and *Atonement* [2007]): a stylish reworking of the Bourne theme with a teenage girl in the lead, and with the fairy-tale mythology up front rather than implicit. The influence of the Bourne template in discussions of contemporary action thrillers, and probably in their production, is indicated by the amount of times the comparison is made in reviews of Wright's film: as in, for example, *Empire*'s summary of *Hanna* as 'a *Bourne*-like action movie [retold] through the rubric of a fable – Hans Christian Andersen refitted with Glocks, smart phones and satellite surveillance'; or as in *Sight & Sound*'s description of the film as 'baby *Bourne*'.

Given the tendency of Hollywood to latch on to concepts and genres for as long as the taste for them endures, there's a temptation to write off this kind of influence as economic opportunism, though this wouldn't account for *why* certain concepts catch on in the first place. It's also significant to what extent the look of these films feels like a distinct response to much contemporary film-making practice. Ian Nathan's *Empire* review of *Hanna* draws attention to the way Wright brings a sensorial vividness to a genre that, in this present century, is usually associated with the synthetic: a reinvestment in the human body, in other words. *Salt* seems unsure at times whether or not it wants to be *Mission: Impossible*, though it's more cartoon-like elements are balanced by a grainy, greyish feel to much of the photography, the now familiar preoccupation with all-pervasive surveillance, and a generally unglamorous turn from Jolie, very different from the slinky sex-bomb look of Lara Croft.

Perhaps the most significant thing about these two films, though, in light of what I discussed in Chapter Six, is the that they are narratives shaped around female characters; a fact that gives their theme of masculine control and identity-shaping a new twist. It's interesting to find out that, before Jolie came on board, *Salt* was originally conceived as a vehicle for *Mission: Impossible* star Tom Cruise. The dwindling star-power of the latter, and Jolie's ascension to the position of world's most powerful female actor, may have had something to do with the film's gender-switch, though it also turns what would have been a standard action flick into something more unusual, and maybe an indication of future trends. The end of 2011, in fact, saw the release of *The Girl with the Dragon Tattoo*, David Fincher's version of Stieg Larsson's first 'Millennium' novel (from a trilogy which has already generated three Swedish-produced films [all 2009]). The trilogy's heroine, a world-class computer hacker called Lisbeth Salander, is one of the most remarkable fictional characters to emerge in years, with a back story and mode of operating that makes Jason Bourne seem a stickler for rules by comparison. If Larsson's controversial creation has elements of male fantasy about her – a masochistic one, perhaps – it is notable that she is a heroine who complicates moral boundaries; a social outcast and a technical genius, working in and through the clandestine spaces of the system.

What J.B. Did Next, Part Two

An even better indication that a film has embedded itself in the cultural imaginary is when, as in the descriptions above of *Hanna*, it lends itself to descriptive shorthand. '*Bourne* meets *Inception*!' yelled British posters for the 2011 film *The Adjustment Bureau*: the type of journalistic conjunction that is both the worst example of film-reviewing style, and an accurate indication of the way such movie concepts appeal to viewers of films, and the people who produce them. With its jaunty foot pursuits around a New York transformed by magic-door geography, and the intrigue of its premise (a team of supernatural bureaucrats, with a fashion sense straight out of 1940s *film noir*, 'adjust' the outcome of human actions to ensure the successful realisation of 'the plan'), George Nolfi's movie – adapted from a story by science-fiction writer Philip K. Dick – shows its debt to the most significant action series of the previous decade, as well as to Christopher Nolan's much-discussed 2010 hit.

It helps, of course, that the film's star, Matt Damon, is now so synonymous with the role of Bourne that his mere presence in a film evokes some aspect of it. Damon's presence clearly encourages this inter-textual reference point – especially useful for *Bourne* producers Universal, who were also behind *The Adjustment Bureau* – which helps sell the film as an idea and, in principle, increase its profitability. Yet the film also reflects the influence of the *Bourne* series in other ways. Writer-director Nolfi, we may remember, co-wrote the screenplay for *Ultimatum*, and *The Adjustment Bureau* shares with the earlier film an interest both in the real-life architecture and labyrinths of the city, and the ways in which individuals can evade the reaches of rule-bound authority. Considering Nolfi's screenwriting pedigree, *The Adjustment Bureau* is ultimately a very slight and oddly non-political film, especially as its main character is a young politician with ambitions for higher office. Its tale of angelic intervention and metaphysical romance (with Damon appearing to choose Emily Blunt's ballet dancer over a shot at the White House) is actually as old-fashioned as the Bureau's tailoring, though this distances the film in a significant way from the superhuman or violent excesses of other recent Hollywood fare.

Many online sources quote Greengrass's joke that the fourth outing for Bourne should be called '*The Bourne Redundancy*'; an indication that, for him, the series had done its work. His next film would appear in some respects a return to his docu-fictional background, and his interest in representing conflict zones and terrorism, yet in some respects it feels like a sequel to *Ultimatum*. *Green Zone* (2010) (Fig 30) is based loosely on Rajiv Chandrasekaran's book *Imperial Life in the Emerald City*, an account of the first year of the US-led occupation of Baghdad ('Green Zone' refers to the heavily-protected enclave within which military and intelligence chiefs planned Iraq's future). The highly anticipated film reunited Greengrass with Damon, who plays Roy Miller, a fictional Chief Warrant Officer in the US army. *Green Zone*'s story, which reduces and simplifies much of its source material, focuses on Miller's frustrated efforts to search for WMD (Weapons of Mass Destruction) in Iraq's capital city. While we initially see Miller operating as a trusting soldier, looking for weapons that keep failing to materialise, his faith in his superiors is gradually eroded. This reaches its peak when an Iraqi with links to a high-profile General, Al-Rawi, a man who may provide information on the existence of WMD, is literally snatched from Miller's hands by Special Forces. The rest of the film shows Miller in his effort to recapture the Iraqi and track down Al-Rawi, in order to shed light on the mystery of the missing weapons.

It's no accident that the marriage of Greengrass's film-making style and Damon's star persona should produce a movie not unlike their *Bourne* outings. If there's anything slightly odd about *Green Zone*, though, it's that it's perhaps *too much* like a *Bourne* film. Miller's change of heart comes about when he realises the truth behind his orders: that he has been searching for nothing, merely a pretext for invasion. His subsequent actions are an attempt both at self-redemption and revealing the truth, and in the process, to expose those who manufacture consent for war through manipulating information. *Green Zone* not only has the action we'd expect of the *Bourne* franchise – the film's main set piece is a breathless car and foot chase between Miller and his Special Forces nemesis, Briggs (Jason Isaacs), to intercept Al-Rawi – but it also has the familiar cast of characters. Lawrie Dayne (Amy Ryan), a conscientious reporter for the *Wall Street Journal*, stands in for Landy (at one point she even repeats Landy's dialogue, claiming that 'this isn't what I signed up for'); she is the one who, at the end of the film, receives Miller's report about the official deception. Clark Poundstone (Greg Kinnear), meanwhile, the chief intelligence agent who supplies Miller with his (mis)information, is a cool modern villain in the line of Noah Vosen, and even shares his fondness for grey suits and rimless glasses. And Miller himself, though he doesn't share Bourne's uncanny instincts, is clearly a well-intentioned innocent caught up in a web of deceit: like Bourne, too, he exits alone, suggesting that the real work is still to do beyond the film itself.

Green Zone is not a bad film at all: as a thriller it works effectively, the action is presented as well as we'd expect, and it also offers a glimpse into the bizarre world of being an occupying army (complete with poolside parties, beer and boom-boxes inside Iraq's royal palaces). What's most interesting, though, is to consider what the movie sets out to do.

Fig 30: Bourne goes to Iraq: Matt Damon stops following orders in *Green Zone*.

Greengrass indicated in a *Guardian* interview that his aim in making an Iraq War movie was, in his words, 'to see if I [could] bring that *Bourne* audience with me'.[73] From one perspective, the idea of transferring Bourne to the combat zone seems a logical one. Greengrass shows his own political agenda, and also his identification with his films' heroes, when he states that *Green Zone* 'was a film made out of my sense of affront and anger. I wanted to say, "I know what you did." And that statement has immeasurably more power if it's made to a broad audience in the vernacular of popular genre cinema'.[74]

This is a commendable intent, but not an easy task. In his detailed study of American movies representing the Iraq War, Martin Barker notes how this group of films – a 'toxic genre', to follow his book's title – have practically all failed to make an impact at the box office; the implication being that audiences are just not prepared to deal with the realities of ongoing conflict on their cinema screens.[75] Even Kathryn Bigelow's *The Hurt Locker* (2008), which in a very significant vote beat Avatar to the Best Picture Oscar in 2010, was seen by comparatively few people – it earned just $12 million at the US box office, compared to *Avatar*'s $760 million! – and therefore made more of a symbolic impression than a real one. That particular movie worked on a very small scale, looking in intimate detail at the routine of a small group of men, and therefore was unlikely to draw in a big audience; *Green Zone*, by contrast, looked to bring some of the epic scale, paranoia and do-or-die action of *Ultimatum* to bear on its subject, with the aim of bringing war into the movie mainstream. Yet *Green Zone*, perhaps surprisingly, also failed to catch on in cinemas, capturing only a fraction of the market that *Ultimatum* managed,[76] and much less critical attention. Might we conclude from this, finally, that 'too much reality' is simply too much for audiences to deal with? If so, how in the end can we understand the supposedly 'serious' intent behind a film like *Ultimatum*?

Footnotes

62. Quoted in Jeff Labreque, 'No Matt Damon in "Bourne Legacy": Report'. Entertainment Weekly Online, 11 October 2010

63. Nick James, 'Syndromes of a New Century', *Sight & Sound* 20.2 (2010), 34–38.

64. James Chapman, *Licence to Thrill: A Cultural History of the James Bond Films*, second edition (London: I.B. Tauris, 2007), p. 243.

65. Chapman, *ibid.*, p. 240.

66. Chapman, *ibid.*, p. 243.

67. Chapman, *ibid.*, p. 242.

68. Chapman, *ibid.*, pp. 65–70.

69. See Geoff King, 'Just Like a Movie?: 9/11 and Hollywood Spectacle', in Geoff King (ed), *The Spectacle of the Real: From Hollywood to 'Reality' TV and Beyond* (Bristol and Portland: Intellect, 2005), pp. 47–58.

70. Chapman (*op cit.*, pp.234–35) points out that 9/11 is referred to obliquely in *Die Another Day*; a film conceived before, but finished after, the attacks.

71. Michael Atkinson, 'All surface, no feeling', *Sight & Sound*, 18.12 (2008), 21–23 (22).

72. Atkinson, *ibid.*

73. Quoted in Steve Rose, 'Paul Greengrass: the betrayal behind *Green Zone*', *Guardian*, 8 March 2010.

74. In Rose, *ibid.*

75. Martin Barker, *A 'Toxic Genre': The Iraq War Films* (London: Pluto Press, 2011).

76. The film, which had an event-movie budget of around $100m, took in just $35m at the US theatrical box office, and £5m in the UK.

Summary and questions

- Films such as *The Bourne Supremacy* and *The Bourne Ultimatum* have probably influenced other film series such as the James Bond movies, as seen in *Casino Royale* and *Quantum of Solace*. However, we should really see this as reflective of changes in the representation of reality in cinema and television more generally, especially after the events of 11 September 2001.

- The proposed 'side-quel' to the *Bourne* movies, *The Bourne Legacy*, indicates the appeal for film-makers, producers and viewers of multi-stranded series.

- Paul Greengrass and Matt Damon's follow-up movie, *Green Zone*, attempted to rework some of the themes of the *Bourne* series into a 'real-world' situation: the war in Iraq. Its lack of success seems to indicate that myths may be dramatically more effective than fact-based drama.

- Does *The Bourne Ultimatum* seem to exist in a 'fictional' or 'real' world? Is there a grey area between fact-based and fictional cinema, as seen in comparisons between *Green Zone* and *Ultimatum*?

- Do fiction films have an ability to explore real-world situations in a way that fact-based narratives do not?

- Does Hollywood 'fantasy' always have to be triumphalist? Can fantasy be used in a way that is still critical or challenging of dominant values and ideas?

Conclusion – Truth and Lies

Thinking about why *Green Zone* failed where *Ultimatum* succeeded may give some insight as to how popular fiction films work – and in turn, how they don't. To do this, we need to go briefly back to the beginning: to the question of where 'serious' ends and 'entertainment' begins, or whether – as I've suggested throughout – the dividing line is not so clear.

In a *Guardian* feature just prior to the release of *Green Zone*, Steve Rose separates Greengrass's *Bourne* movies from his other work, suggesting that the director brings a sense of intense realism not just to his fact-based dramas, but to 'far-fetched popcorn movies'.[77] The problem with making this distinction is that it sounds self-contradictory. If, as Rose suggests, Greengrass's so-called popcorn movies 'were shot through with real post-9/11 paranoias', doesn't this in fact make *Ultimatum*, at some level, just as 'real' a film as *United 93*, and certainly not 'far-fetched'? Most movies invite us to believe in the world they depict. What really matters is how convincing the movies are, and what ideas they provoke in us. Jason Bourne does not exist, but the story shown on screen *suggests* a world which, if not necessarily true, we can at least recognise aspects of in our own lives. The *Bourne* films therefore indicate the power of cinematic storytelling to create real-world impressions: they may have a more powerful sense of reality *because* they seem to describe a hidden and complex world.

United 93 is actually closer to *Ultimatum* than might initially seem the case, even if its ultimate effect is more harrowing than heroic. The dreadful fascination of *United 93* is that it depicts events we can only imagine but never know: the film and its viewers therefore fill the gaps that demand to be filled. A problem with *Green Zone* is that, by 2010, most of the controversial facts surrounding the Iraq invasion were well discussed. Like any film based on real, recent events, this causes a problem: either the film tells us what we already know and believe, or in contrast, it sells us a series of fictions posing as truths. Unexpectedly, it was the same soldier on whom the character of Miller is based, Richard Gonzales, who publicly rejected the film's relationship to the actual truth, suggesting *Green Zone* should not be seen as 'anything other than a great Hollywood action thriller'.[78] Evidence has since come to light that the film might prove more accurate than Gonzales initially believed; a fact which might help *Green Zone*'s long-term reputation.[79] Yet the film remains an example of the difficulties involved in mixing factual material with a mainstream fictional form. By trimming the source material to ensure feature length and plot structure, in fact, the film may fall short of the known facts and complexity, and may paradoxically come across as *less* real than a pure fiction film.

Green Zone may have proved more powerful, in other words, if it hadn't made so many claims to truth; especially when its fictions later turned out to be closer to fact. It is maybe the freedoms offered by the fiction film, then, and the space it leaves for our imagination, that allow it to feel real. The appeal of 'conspiracy' thrillers such as *Ultimatum*, in fact, is the way they offer a fantasy of the real, but a fantasy that seems highly credible within a world of political uncertainty, manipulation, and distrust. Many critics of Hollywood cinema write it off as pure wish-fulfilment or an advert for the American capitalist dream; in doing this, they ignore the possibility for the conspiracy film's inversion of this wish, and the possible delights in visualising the world *not* in the way that adverts or politicians reassure us it is.

This is still a kind of fantasy, but clearly a seductive one for many viewers: the feeling of speculating or working out how things *really* work, behind the 'real' images we see, for example, in our mainstream news media. We can see this if we take note of some of the films to come out in the years following *Ultimatum*'s release, and which to some extent show the abiding influence of the *Bourne* series on modern film-making. The shape of popular political cinema in the coming years, and the relevance of the *Bourne* series to it, remains to be seen: it may depend as much on the choices made in the corridors of power, as much as those ideas hatched in the studios of Hollywood.

Footnotes

77. Rose, *op cit.*

78. Richard Gonzales, 'The Truth About "Green Zone"', FOXNews.com, 13 March 2010.

79. See Alex von Tunzelman, 'Green Zone: A Surfeit of Sincerity', *Guardian*, 1 September 2011.

Bibliography: suggestions for further reading

Books and articles

Michael Atkinson, 'All surface, no feeling', *Sight & Sound*, 18.12 (2008), 21–23

Martin Barker, *A Toxic Genre: The Iraq War Films*, London: Pluto Press, 2011

David Bordwell, *Narration in the Fiction Film*, London: Methuen, 1985

David Bordwell, *The Way Hollywood Tells It: Story and Style in Modern Movies*, Berkeley: University of California Press, 2006

Scott Bukatman, *Matters of Gravity: Special Effects and Supermen in the Twentieth Century*, Durham: Duke University Press, 2003

James Chapman, *Licence to Thrill: A Cultural History of the James Bond Films*, second edition, London: I.B. Tauris, 2007

J. Hoberman, 'Unquiet Americans', *Sight & Sound*, 16.10 (2006), 20–23

Ali Jaafar, 'Casualties of War', *Sight & Sound*, 18.2 (2008), 16–22

Geoff King, *Spectacular Narratives: Hollywood in the Age of the Blockbuster*, London and New York: I.B. Tauris, 2000

Rob McInnes, *Action/Adventure Films: A Teacher's Guide*, revised edition, Leighton Buzzard: Auteur, 2010

Richard Maltby, *Hollywood Cinema*, second edition, Malden, Oxford, Melbourne and Berlin: Blackwell, 2003

John Silberg, 'Bourne Again', *American Cinematographer*, 88.9 (September 2007) http://www.theasc.com/ac_magazine/September2007/TheBourneUltimatum/page1.php [Accessed 7 January 2012]

Tom Shone, *Blockbuster: How the Jaws and Jedi Generation Turned Hollywood into a Boom-Town*, London: Simon and Schuster, 2004

Yvonne Tasker (ed.), *Action and Adventure Cinema*, London and New York: Routledge, 2004

Kristin Thompson, *Storytelling in Film and Television*, Cambridge and London: Harvard University Press, 2003

Reviews and interviews

Peter Bradshaw, review of *The Bourne Ultimatum*, *Guardian*, 17th August 2007 http://www.guardian.co.uk/film/2007/aug/17/actionandadventure.mattdamon?INTCMP=SRCH [Accessed 7 January 2012]

Manohla Dargis, 'Still Searching, but With Darker Eyes', *New York Times*, 3rd August 2007 http://movies.nytimes.com/2007/08/03/movies/03bour.html [Accessed 7 January 2012]

David Denby, 'War Wounds', *The New Yorker*, 6 August 2007 http://www.newyorker.com/arts/critics/cinema/2007/08/06/070806crci_cinema_denby [Accessed 7 January 2012]

Philip French, review of *The Bourne Ultimatum*, *Observer*, 19th August 2007 http://www.guardian.co.uk/film/2007/aug/19/mattdamon.actionandadventure?INTCMP=SRCH [Accessed 7 January 2012]

Jeff Labreque, 'No Matt Damon in "Bourne Legacy": Report'. *Entertainment Weekly* Online, October 11th 2010 http://news-briefs.ew.com/2010/10/11/no-matt-damon-in-bourne-legacy/ [Accessed 7 January 2012]

Demetrios Matheou, review of *The Bourne Ultimatum*, *Sight & Sound*, 17.10 (2007), 50–51

John Patterson, 'Killer Instinct', *Guardian*, 6 August 2007 http://www.guardian.co.uk/film/2007/aug/06/television1?INTCMP=SRCH [Accessed 7 January 2012]

Steve Rose, 'Paul Greengrass: the betrayal behind *Green Zone*', *Guardian*, 8 March 2010 http://www.guardian.co.uk/film/2010/mar/08/paul-greengrass-betrayal-green-zone?INTCMP=SRCH [Accessed 7 January 2012]

Filmography: suggestions for further viewing

The Adjustment Bureau (dir. George Nolfi, 2011)

All the President's Men (dir. Alan J. Pakula, 1976)

Bloody Sunday (dir. Paul Greengrass, 2002)

The Bourne Identity (dir. Doug Liman, 2002)

The Bourne Supremacy (dir. Paul Greengrass, 2004)

Casino Royale (dir. Martin Campbell, 2006)

The Dark Knight (dir. Christopher Nolan, 2008)

Die Another Day (dir. Lee Tamahori, 2002)

Die Hard 4.0 (dir. Len Wiseman, 2007)

The French Connection (dir. William Friedkin, 1971)

The Fugitive (dir. Andrew Davis, 1993)

The Girl with the Dragon Tattoo (dir. David Fincher, 2011)

Green Zone (dir. Paul Greengrass, 2010)

Hanna (dir. Joe Wright, 2011)

The Ipcress File (dir. Sidney J. Furie, 1965)

North by Northwest (dir. Alfred Hitchcock, 1959)

The Parallax View (dir. Alan J. Pakula, 1974)

Quantum of Solace (dir. Marc Forster, 2008)

Salt (dir. Philip Noyce, 2010)

The Thirty-Nine Steps (dir. Alfred Hitchcock, 1935)

United 93 (dir. Paul Greengrass, 2006)

Index